RAISE
YOUR SQ

RAISE YOUR SQ

How The Power of Spiritual Intelligence

Can Change Your Life in 7 Days

ANNIE RIDOUT

RADAR

First published in Great Britain in 2023 by Radar, an imprint of
Octopus Publishing Group Ltd
Carmelite House
50 Victoria Embankment
London EC4Y 0DZ
www.octopusbooks.co.uk

An Hachette UK Company
www.hachette.co.uk

First published in paperback in 2024

Distributed in the US by Hachette Book Group
1290 Avenue of the Americas
4th and 5th Floors
New York, NY 10104

Distributed in Canada by Canadian Manda Group
664 Annette Street, Toronto, Ontario, Canada M6S 2C8

ISBN: 978-1-80419-129-3

A CIP catalogue record for this book is available from the British Library.

Printed and bound in the UK.

1 3 5 7 9 10 8 6 4 2

Typeset in 11/15pt Sabon LT Pro by Jouve (UK), Milton Keynes

This FSC® label means that materials used
for the product have been responsibly sourced.

MIX
Paper | Supporting
responsible forestry
FSC® C104740

For my mum, Julia Davies, who gently guided me towards spirituality. And my dad, Kerk Davies, whose innate spirituality is contagious.

CONTENTS

INTRODUCTION

I was sitting in the basement of a Scandi-inspired London workspace one Saturday in the summer of 2019, on a day retreat. There were white walls, stone floors and both potted and hanging plants. Outside, the sun was beating down on the City of London's quiet weekend streets and we were gathered around a large table in a cool, dark room. There was incense burning. I was there with fourteen other women to learn about how to find more joy and pleasure in our lives.

The day had started awkwardly, as the venue had been double-booked. But Tamu, the leader of the retreat, kept her calm. She took some deep breaths and figured out how we could share the space with a rowdy hen party. It was decided that we'd work down in the basement and they could have the upstairs space.

As we sat at that table, waiting quietly for the leader to begin the session, the silence was broken by R&B singer Erykah Badu booming from a sound system upstairs. The hen party hadn't yet arrived and we had no idea who'd turned it on. We all laughed. One woman said: "I wonder what that means?" And in that moment, I realized that I was surrounded by women who felt like I did: that in life, you are presented with unexplained occurrences and it's up to you to find their meaning.

Up until then, I'd been manically trying to balance my freelance writing career – as a journalist, author and editor of a digital magazine – with raising my young children. Every month,

I'd earn just enough money to pay my half of the bills. But it felt tight, stressful and my anxiety levels were pretty high. To add to that, I was now heavily pregnant with my third baby, meaning I'd soon have three children under the age of five to flex my career around. I had no idea how it was going to work; I'd done very little planning. I wanted three children, I wanted to have a career and I needed to be earning more money.

Two things happened on that retreat.

Firstly, I got clear on what I wanted from my career: a better work-life balance (working fewer hours, for sure); a lot more money flowing in each month; and for the online course business I'd just launched to grow, meaning that I'd have a steady income stream and my husband could quit his job to help me with both the business and the kids.

Secondly – and perhaps more importantly – I reconnected with my spiritual self. I was raised by a spiritual mother who encouraged me to use oracle cards to make big life decisions, touched wood in superstition and taught me about the power of intuition. The retreat was a welcome reminder that it is not only okay, but actually incredibly powerful, to visualize success and work towards it. I decided to go home, dig out my tarot and oracle cards once again and to re-engage with the positive superstitions with which I was raised. I was already "vision-boarding" – making a tangible collage of pictures of my hopes and dreams (we'll go into this in more depth later, see page 80) – when it came to not only my everyday life, but more specifically, my working life. I just hadn't given it a name yet. From that point on, I started to actively and unashamedly incorporate spirituality into my working life. I quickly realized that raising my spiritual intelligence – my SQ – would help me manifest the life I wanted.

Let me explain what I mean by "spirituality", because I don't necessarily mean connecting to one specific god or religion. I'm not religious. I'm open to the teachings of organized religions, but

I don't attend a specific setting to learn or pray and I don't believe there is just one higher power dictating what happens in our lives. Rather, to me, spirituality is about being open to the possibility that there may be something beyond the body and mind; an energy we can access but that isn't visible. You just need an open mind, a desire for some magic in your life and the understanding that, sometimes, it can be hugely comforting to feel supported by a power that you can't see or hear but that you can simply sense all around you; for instance, when out in nature, or when creative ideas land in your head.

We might view spirituality as a way to connect with the world around us. For example, have you ever entered a forest or stepped on to a beautiful beach and felt an inner ecstasy? It's like your belly is doing a little flip of excitement because it's just so lovely to be there. In that moment, you're connecting to nature and I'd describe that as a spiritual connection with your surroundings. It's as if that relationship to the Earth and the natural world activates your soul.

Some of the world's greatest leaders have been relying on SQ to raise their game for years. Oprah Winfrey uses it, with daily gratitude journaling and prayer. Bestselling writer Elizabeth Gilbert wrote a book – *Big Magic* – on the subject. Researcher, writer and author Brené Brown believes we are all connected by a power greater than ourselves. Throughout this book, I have incorporated interviews with leading figures across a range of industries who generously shared their personal SQ practices, how they incorporate spirituality into their working lives, their reading recommendations and the story of where it all began for them.

In terms of using SQ to drive my own career success, once I'd reconnected to my spirituality, all those dreams I uncovered on that day retreat started to come into fruition. I got back into manifesting, collecting gemstones to use for meditating on my goals and lighting candles for magic spells that would bring greater success. And off the back of this, my online course business – helping women to launch their own online businesses – boomed. I started turning over £10,000 a month rather than struggling to make £2,000. Over the following months, even that figure doubled.

My husband quit his job to help me run the business and raise the kids. Our work-life balance became blissful. We had morning coffee meetings while our newborn napped in the buggy; delicious, healthy lunches at home; afternoon walks; bursts of marketing to let people know about the courses; then we'd be off to collect the kids from school.

I remember, after the first week of December 2019, deciding to take the rest of the month off. We went away to the countryside with the kids and had an idyllic break, away from the hustle and bustle of the city. Money was coming in fairly effortlessly (obviously we worked hard, but only sat at desks for a few hours a day). Having these new spiritual tools was giving me an inner confidence. I knew that if I stayed clear on what I wanted – and believed it was possible – it would be.

And then three months later, the pandemic hit, suddenly making our work and home lives intrinsically linked. I was already working online from home, but not with three children around me. However, we'd set up a business that we could take turns to work on and we felt so lucky about our set-up. Financially, we were flying. And if I needed to "escape" (without leaving the home), I could meditate using a candle, call for help from the deities I was already praying to in my mind – asking how to keep the sales rolling in, or to regain a sense of calm – or light incense and waft it around my home office to remove the negative energy I could sense after a conversation with a difficult customer.

Most of us are well-versed in the importance of a healthy body and mind, but spirit matters, too. Those with a high SQ focus on what they want across the board. They don't move through life feeling negative and complaining about their lot. They focus on what brings them joy and they ask for more of it, whether that's rest, creativity, movement or money. Whatever it is, they believe they deserve it. Their eyes are always looking for new and exciting opportunities. They exude success and that's because they've achieved it. Some call it a "manifesting mindset"; I call it raising your SQ.

It's important to be clear that, when I talk about achieving "success", I don't necessarily mean the accumulation of greater wealth. Success might mean a better balance between time at home and time at work. It might come from doing work that feels more meaningful or gives your life more purpose. But if we are able to feel financially comfortable (which definitely matters) while doing that meaningful work, well, that's a good place to aim for.

If you're ready to feel more fulfilled with your work life, to reach for what you'd love but perhaps feel is currently out of your grasp, you need to increase your SQ. And this book will teach you how to do that. I'm not going to suggest you start to pray to a god you don't believe in or attend any kind of religious place or ceremonies. I will just ask you to be open to new ideas. Because an open and curious mind leads to a more creative and fulfilling life.

I'll walk you through each of my spiritual practices, including tarot, mantras, gemstones, incantations, being guided by intuition and superstition, manifesting and sage-smudging. I'll be looking at the history of these rituals, some with origins in organized religions, others associated more with witchcraft, tribal practices and occultism. And I'll be showing you how they can be incorporated into the modern world in a way that works for you.

I've used magic spells to make more sales and oracle cards to help me price up a job. I've manifested pretty much my entire life using vision boards to list my desires. I use scent diffusers to bring positive energy in at the beginning of each working day and burn sage around my office space to dispel negative energy after difficult work encounters. And each night, before bed, I write a list of everything I feel grateful for.

But I also work hard on a practical level, as a freelancer, business owner, journalist and author. For real work-life satisfaction, I believe you need a combination of magic and sweat.

And for anyone who is cynical about "manifesting" (especially in terms of things being somewhat easier to "manifest" when coming from a place of privilege, which is definitely true), it might be useful to reframe your understanding of manifesting. It's not simply about visualizing something, then sitting back and waiting for it to happen. Instead, it's about getting clear on what you want and working towards that. Because if you don't know what you want, you won't be able to take the necessary steps to bring it to fruition.

While I ask that you read this book with an open mind, I understand that some of the rituals and practices I tell you about may seem wacky or weird. I know people are sometimes critical about anything that isn't tangible, or provable by science, so I'll be speaking to the cynics among you as well as those who are ready and willing to listen, learn and make changes. I'm here to lighten the concept of spirituality, to debunk common misconceptions and to show you how raising your SQ can improve your life.

I'll show you how creating rituals can add a touch of magic to your life, as well as help with practical work matters. We'll explore the use of tarot cards to guide decision making and how to light a candle each evening while you say positive career affirmations out loud. I'll guide you through how to harness the power of gemstones when you need an energy boost mid-afternoon, as well as how to use movement to generate fresh ideas.

Importantly, many of these spiritual practices will cost you nothing. I'll recommend some of the physical tools I use (such as tarot cards, gemstones and candles) but it is mostly down to you, your mind and the magical energy surrounding you.

You can use this book as a spiritual toolkit. It will help you to work out what you really want from your working life and how to get it. There are tools for activating your intuition, rather than feeling flummoxed at the very thought of just going with your instinct. The practices I suggest will give you the confidence to follow your heart sometimes, instead of your mind. They will help you to reignite your creativity. And they will encourage you to throw out the rule book and instead be guided by your spiritual intelligence. Your SQ.

1

WHAT IS SQ?

Spirit (n.) ORIGIN: Latin *spiritus* "breath, spirit", from *spirare* "breathe".

My spiritual upbringing

When I was born, in the mid-1980s, my mum had me christened. She'd been raised in London by Irish immigrant parents – her mother was a cleaner, her father laid tennis courts – who belonged to the Roman Catholic church. Aged 15, my mum and her older brother Jim decided it was more fun to be out with their mates around London's edgy Portobello Market than at church, so they rather rebelliously stopped attending. That was the end of my mum's formal relationship with the church, but she retained an on-off belief in there being a "god" of some sort.

So when, some 14 years later, my older sister was born and taken immediately into intensive care, my mum found herself praying that she would be okay. She made a deal with God: if you save my baby, I'll have her christened. Like most mothers, she would have done anything – mainstream or alternative medicine, or spiritual – to save her baby. I discovered this myself when my own baby became seriously ill . . . but more on that later. Fortunately, my sister was soon healthy and allowed to go home. Mum stuck to her word and had her christened. And when I was born, two and a half years later, Mum thought she better get me christened too, as a form of protection. My younger brother, too. But that was where religion, in its more formal sense, started and ended for us as children.

We didn't go to church, except for the odd Christmas Eve service, or popping in to light a candle for people we'd lost and to admire the beautiful stained glass. But my parents still instilled in us some of the same values that others are taught through religion: to look out for others, to have hope and a positive mindset, to believe in ourselves and our capabilities, to practise gratitude and to accept others just as they are, to belong to a community and to celebrate and come together for ceremonies. These are values that I am carrying through to my children, the next generation. And they span both home and working life.

Alongside these values, there always remained the casual knowledge that, as a family, we were surrounded by the spirits of people who'd passed. I now understand that this is on the more unusual side, but back then, it was just normal. I remember when an old friend of mine came round one afternoon, when I was about 15, and, as she entered the hallway, she asked: "What's that smell?" Mum, Dad and I started sniffing to see if we could work out what she was talking about and we all noticed a strong, lovely fragrance permeating the air. My mum pointed to an oil diffuser on the corner table next to us all and said: "It's coming from there." She explained that she and one of her treasured friends, Isabella, had bought the oil together in Paris, where Isabella lived. Isabella had passed away only a few months earlier and, without needing to articulate it, we all understood – Mum, Dad and me – that this scent suddenly filling the air was a connection to Isabella's spirit. She wanted us to know that she was still with us, in some way.

If you weren't raised with these beliefs, or have never considered whether a person's soul or "energy" remains once they have passed away, that might sound a bit out-there. I understand. Because I grew up with it, it's completely normal for me, but I know that there is an element of perception here, as well as what we choose to see, believe and understand about life, death and spirit. As my siblings and I grew older, my mum became a bereavement counsellor, so we have always had open conversations about death; it's not a taboo subject for us. Perhaps my mother was more able to go into this difficult profession because of her spiritual beliefs. Either way, talking about life, death, birth and spirituality was ordinary for us.

So it didn't feel particularly unusual when my mum sent me off, aged 16, to study reiki, a form of energy healing that originated in Japan. It was just me, my friend Lizzie and five other older women. We learned about chakras (seven sacred areas on the body) and the different ways we can use our hands to heal: either by touching the skin, or hovering them just above the body, over the chakras.

I found myself wanting to heal people, to try out my new reiki skills. I remember laying my sister down one afternoon when she was feeling ill and practising reiki on her. She said it felt like my hands were emanating an energy that was being transferred to her body. The idea with reiki – and most energy healing – is that the healer is guiding the client's body to heal itself, so the body will take whatever it needs. My sister sat up after the session and noted that her back was no longer aching. It wasn't what she'd wanted the session for – she had a cold – but she was quite impressed with this unexpected benefit. I continued to practise reiki on people close to me, but I didn't talk about it widely, as it wasn't what most of my teenage friends were doing at that time. Instead, it became one of my secret SQ tools.

Put simply, SQ is about having the knowledge, and belief, that something exists beyond body and mind. Something bigger than us. More powerful. An energy, or higher being, that can guide us, support us and make our time on Earth more magical. In order to access this, or firm up our belief, we can experiment with different treatments (such as reiki), as well as simply keeping our eyes open for signs that might guide us on our way.

We hold many of the answers we need in our own subconscious minds, but, sometimes, a little nudge from an outside source can help to shift those answers into our conscious minds. That outside source might be "God" or "the Universe" or "Source". It might be the sighting of a white feather, a penny or an unusual bird. It might appear in a dream; after all, dreams have long been associated with spirituality, particularly lucid dreaming, where a sleeping person manages to control what is happening in their dream. In fact, a study into lucid dreaming and spirituality suggested that "dreaming itself can be considered a spiritual practice"[1].

In these times of disconnection and isolation, it feels increasingly important that we connect with each other, with the land and with the idea that not everything has been – or needs to be – "proven" for it to feel real to us as individuals. We need to be able to dream. Dreaming is mind-expanding, creative and helps us to find our way forward.

---

[1] "The Luminous Night of the Soul: The Relationship between Lucid Dreaming and Spirituality", Tadas Stumbrys, *International Journal of Transpersonal Studies*, vol. 40, issue 2, 2021

MY SQ JOURNEY

Sharmadean Reid MBE is a British Jamaican entrepreneur. She is the founder of WAH Nails and Beautystack and an advocate for women's empowerment.

I was raised in a spiritual home, my family were Seventh-day Adventists, so church was very much present in our house. But it wasn't a strict household: some members of the family went to church every week, or even several times a week, and others didn't. My grandad didn't go to church until he was in his fifties, but my grandma attended from when she was 18. She was the spiritual leader of the family.

Since then, lots of my aunties have become involved in church: not just attending, they partake in the business of church, running the treasury. Seventh-day Adventism is a bit like Christianity and Judaism mixed together, so I still don't eat pork or prawns and we have sabbath from Friday sunset to Saturday sunset. But most of the church's teachings are similar to those of Christianity. One of the key elements of Seventh-day Adventism teaching is the idea of a clean body and mind.

I would go to church every week as a child – and I absolutely loved it – but then, when I was 13, I went to something called a Revelation Seminar, like a Bible class for anyone who wants to go deep on the Book of Revelation. I'd go after school and we'd work on a theological analysis of the Book of Revelation . . . and I just found it really weird. It was all "fire and brimstone, we're all going to burn in hell, Catholics are the Devil". It was full of fear and judgement. Something clicked and I thought: I don't want to go to church any more . . . and I just stopped going. But then I found myself constantly searching for a new religion, because, at that age, I didn't really understand the difference between "faith" and "religion". I just assumed they were one and the same. From the age of 13 to 22, I would attend a Catholic church, then a Buddhist temple. I'd research Jainism, which is probably the closest to what I believe now.

But what I have settled on, after all those years of research and reading, is that actually I just believe in the spirit of the Universe and of Mother Nature. And if I subscribe to a religion, it's that: a belief in life forms and the Universe in a part-scientific way – after all, energy comes down to physics and atoms – plus how that energy can affect us as these tiny little specks of humans in the Universe. If all of us got together and labelled this belief system, it would be the same as a religion. But I can have a singular connection to what I believe in and that connection doesn't necessarily have to be reinforced through communal experience and ritual. It can be – and that's nice – but it doesn't have to be.

Nature is my number one connection to spirit. The problem with where I live now is that I'm not near any trees and it drives me a bit mad. I'm moving house and there are going to be trees outside my window; I think that's really important. There are so many studies that show if patients in hospital have a room with a window and a connection to nature, they literally recover faster than patients who don't. So this is what I mean when I say what I believe in is the essence of the Universe, Mother Nature and so on.

Visioning

Every January, I practise visioning, though not through vision-boarding (see page 80). Instead, I write a narrative; I write out the story of me. I include everything from the future that I want in my present. There's a set of about 50 questions that I answer and I use a technique of writing them in the present tense and in the first person. I do that at the start of the year, then I check it halfway through the year, to see my progress.

Spiritual rituals

Every Saturday morning I take a Jivamukti yoga class. This type of yoga contains a sort of sermon: the leader gives a short talk before you do the yoga. Effectively, she is the closest thing to a "guru" that I have. She is so incredible, so wise and very accepting of her own mistakes. I just love it. I light something – sage, a candle or palo santo (sacred wood) – and then I make my coffee and start my yoga.

I also practise transcendental meditation on Saturday afternoons. I had a lesson with a guru, then took a week's meditation course and got my private mantra. Now I use it in my meditation and it's game-changing. Everyone says about meditation, "Oh, this is boring." Then they do it and realize: "Oh, this works."

SQ experiences

I like to take part in spiritual experiences, but I don't follow any particular pattern with them. Two weeks ago I took part in a rebirthing session, where you do intense breathwork (see page 24) for one hour and have an intense experience. I've also done cacao-drinking ceremonies (see page 128). I undertook hypnotherapy and used it to change some of the things my subconscious was saying, even if I didn't believe it in my conscious mind. I've gone foraging with a rasta woman in a forest. I also went to the forest with one of Bear Grylls's apprentices and they taught me how to make fire from scratch. I do these things pretty randomly, as I feel the need. It's the reconnection with myself that they offer me which is so valuable.

Also, I like to push my limits. If I'm going through stressful times, I can stop and remind myself that I can make fire, so I'm not going to die if I'm left alone in the woods. That's actually quite liberating.

SQ books I'd recommend

The Women's History of the World *by Rosalind Miles*

This is all about the fact that women have not had their history written about them properly, ever, from ancient mythology to today. As you read it, you think about how – when you do know your history – what you are doing becomes a divine right. I am descended from Punjabi princesses and African queens: it is my divine right to be doing what I'm doing.

The Myth of Sisyphus *by Albert Camus*

A book all about suicide and why we might be on this Earth. It's not a spiritual book, but I can see spirituality in it. I think that most literature can be spiritual. After all, what is spirituality if not humanity? And what is literature if not tales of humanity? Whatever I read, I'll take what I need from it. I might use an element of it to figure out my manifestation practice.

SQ IN THE WORKPLACE: A BRIEF INTRODUCTION

While my mum has been a more overt influence on me, in terms of spirituality, the way that I bring the spiritual into the workplace has also been inspired by my dad. He ran an independent chain of opticians and I observed him at work throughout my childhood and teens, especially when he got me working on the reception desk of his local shop on Saturdays. While I didn't know it then, he took a spiritual approach to running his business. He treated both his employees and customers with kindness and always kept an open mind. He listened intently, respected everyone around him and had – and continues to have – an abundance of optimism. He seemed to have this ongoing inner faith in himself and what he could achieve and that is how he came to grow his business so that, financially, we became comfortable as a family. He'd had no handouts to get him started, just a clear vision and the belief that he could realize it.

One of his favourite quotes to share with me, when there is something frustrating happening (a difficult customer, say, or my toddler having a tantrum) comes from spiritual leader the Dalai Lama and is along the lines of "I thank you for giving me the opportunity to practise my patience." We laugh, but there is an important lesson there: you may not be able to change what is happening, but why not use it as an opportunity to work on staying calm in the face of adversity? This is all wrapped up with spirituality: taking deep breaths, stilling the mind, staying in the present, being the best version of yourself.

When I was 18, I packed a backpack and went off to travel around India and Thailand for six months. I'd heard about people "finding themselves" in India, but that wasn't why I was going there. I just wanted an adventure and new experiences and it was so wildly different to my life in London that it felt like the right place to go. During those months I was away, my dad was speaking to a family friend. He said to her: "I'm looking forward to getting to know Annie again, when she gets home." He had travelled these countries in his youth and he knew what it could do to you; how it opened your mind.

I did come back changed. I'd immersed myself in the culture – and overt spirituality – of both India and Thailand. I spoke with people about their beliefs and visited temples and places of worship, including the Taj Mahal. I stayed in Varanasi, on the bank of the Ganges, where dead bodies are marched through the town and then lowered on to the river, where they float ceremoniously. How can you not be moved by – and feel connected to – spiritual experiences such as that?

The more you open yourself up to new spiritual experiences, the better placed you will be to recognize the value of raising your SQ. And you don't need to go to India, there are spiritual experiences to be had right on your doorstep. Within your home, even. I'd be willing to make a bet that, as your SQ rises, you will no longer question the value of it. Instead, you'll simply enjoy the meaning, purpose, connection, creativity and magic it brings. I'm seeing this happen with my husband, as I talk more about my own SQ and the different ways I raise and activate it. At first, he wasn't at all interested. "I'm not spiritual," he'd say. "And I don't want to be." In time, though, he started to listen and observe. Now, he is joining me in some of my practices.

We are all spiritual. It's just that some of us embrace it, while others push it away. Channelling spirituality into my everyday life was – and remains – normal for me, but I appreciate that others may feel daunted or embarrassed by some of the practices I'm going to share. Try to remember that, for thousands of years, people have been relying on spiritual practices to help them heal from illness and manifest an improved reality: for example, finding a new romantic partner, or greater financial wealth.

The idea of manifesting has roots as far back as the seventh century BCE, when Siddhartha Gautama, the Buddha, is believed to have said: "All that we are is a result of what we have thought." And so, while "manifesting" is trending on TikTok and becoming increasingly mainstream, this idea that the secret to our destiny begins in the imagination is not new. We need to think it, focus on it, do the work, persevere . . . and then patiently watch as it comes into being.

Moreover, we ought to see spirituality less as a trend and more as being crucial for our general wellbeing in terms of the health of both people and the planet. A psychology study[2] into the relationship between spirituality, health-related behaviour and psychological wellbeing concluded that spirituality is directly related with psychological wellbeing. "Spirituality showed a positive relationship with health-related behaviours," wrote the authors Bożek, Nowak and Blukacz, referring to how spiritual beliefs lead people towards making better choices around their health, such as practising good nutrition habits and having a positive attitude. Another meta-analysis[3] – which looked at hundreds of previous studies linking spirituality with health – revealed there is "ample evidence that religion/spirituality is related to better mental health: less depression, lower stress, less anxiety, greater wellbeing and more positive emotions."

There is also evidence that spirituality plays a part in the health of our planet. It helps us to connect with the Earth and our surroundings and to approach the climate emergency with

---

[2]   "The Relationship Between Spirituality, Health-Related Behavior, and Psychological Well-Being", Agnieszka Bożek, Paweł F Nowak and Mateusz Blukacz, *Frontiers in Psychology*, vol. 11, 14 August 2020

[3]   "Religion, Spirituality, and Health: The Research and Clinical Implications", Harold G Koenig, *ISRN Psychiatry*, vol. 2012, 16 December 2012

hope and optimism rather than eco-anxiety, which can paralyse us into inaction[4].

But look, this is the big stuff and we can work towards that. Really, the route into spirituality – and raising your SQ – begins with mindset. So all I will ask, initially, is that you are ready to open your mind, get curious, hone in on what it is that you want and to believe that it is possible.

Don't worry, I'll help with all of the above in the coming chapters. I'm a qualified life and career coach and have worked with thousands of women over the past few years, through a combination of online courses and coaching. I've encouraged them to believe that their dreams can absolutely come true with a blend of creating a vision, setting clear goals and keeping the faith. I can do the same for you, too.

Once we are clear on the mindset aspect, the next step up is spirit. And this is where it all gets wonderfully "woo woo". We will explore ways to elevate your belief by leaning on energies, or powers, outside of your body and mind. This is what I call spirit. Some people like the term "God" or "higher being". Perhaps, while reading this book, you'll come up with a term that sits comfortably with you. It's also okay to use different terms, depending on how you're feeling or what you're talking about.

Remember, there are no rules. Unlike with organized religions, spirituality is very personal and open to interpretation. You get to pick and choose the bits that work for you and drop those that don't. It's about getting to know yourself better, doing some inner work, connecting with your own thoughts and ideas, your intuition, getting creative and then reaching out – beyond what

---

4   "The Links Between Spirituality and Climate Change", Rita D Sherma, yesmagazine.org, 15 March 2022

you can see, hear, feel – to allow that God/higher being/energy/ Mother Earth/Source to lift you higher.

Ultimately, it needs to feel exciting, because raising your SQ is about improving your life and bringing in more of the good stuff. When you are more spiritually connected, life feels lighter. You discover joy in the tiny everyday things that you might otherwise overlook; you set what might feel like outrageous work goals and truly believe you are worthy of achieving them; you believe in the power of creativity and of connecting with nature.

Raising your SQ doesn't need to be a serious affair: on the contrary, it's all about having fun. As the American actress, musician and songwriter Zooey Deschanel says: "Humour is a part of spirituality." And it is. Becoming spiritually intelligent will improve your home life, working life and personal relationships. It will add joy to your life, laughter, more sensuality and greater work success.

"Just as a candle cannot burn without fire, man cannot live without a spiritual life." Buddha

SQ in the world
Musicians on SQ

I write music on piano and guitar and I'm fascinated by the song-writing processes of famous musicians. Often, they will say they can't explain how an idea lands. Sometimes they will credit a spiritual source for "giving them" the idea; making them the musician through which this great song had to be channelled.

"Well, I don't ever really sit down at the piano and say, 'Right, I've got to write a song now.' I feel a few things and I have ideas. It's very hard to explain but there are always various ideas going through my head."[5]

Freddie Mercury, of Queen

"I think being really connected to a higher power, of having a spirituality, has been really good for me and I pray all the time."

Alicia Keys

"The real power behind whatever success I have now was something I found within myself – something that's in all of us, I think, a little piece of God just waiting to be discovered."

Tina Turner

[5] "'I can dream up all kinds of things' – a classic Freddie Mercury interview from the vaults", Caroline Coon, theguardian.com, 22 November 2011

"I believe in God, but not as one thing, not as an old man in the sky. I believe that what people call God is something in all of us. I believe that what Jesus and Mohammed and Buddha and all the rest said was right. It's just that the translations have gone wrong."

John Lennon

"Music is the mediator between the spiritual and the sensual life."

Ludwig van Beethoven

"I experienced, by the grace of God, a spiritual awakening which was to lead me to a richer, fuller, more productive life."[6]

John Coltrane

"I'm a spiritual kinda guy. I'm not wearing a sheet and walking down the street banging a tambourine . . . And I'm not turning into f***ing Bono. It's private. But I'm connected, man. To something."[7]

Liam Gallagher

"Wake up and live."

Bob Marley

---

[6] *A Love Supreme* liner notes
[7] "Liam Gallagher on life after Oasis", Michael Odell, thetimes.co.uk, 9 April 2011

SQ EXPERIENCE: BREATHWORK

When I first heard about "breathwork", I didn't like the sound of it. How could "work" be calming? I wanted to just relax and receive if I was having any kind of therapy (massage, reiki and so on). But then I had a breathwork session with Claire Frances, a breathwork practitioner, and it blew my mind.

This session started with me sitting cross-legged and breathing "normally": in through the nose, out through the mouth. Then we moved on to conscious connected breath, which is where inhalation and exhalation are connected with no pause in between. At this stage, Claire guided me to lie down on some cushions. She put on music and I was encouraged to breathe with the rhythm of the music, crescendoing my breath as the music picked up pace, then slowing it down again.

My body was tingling all over, as though I'd taken drugs. It was the most powerful mind–body-spirit experience I have ever had while totally sober. My thoughts floated away to my maternal lineage, to the relationship between me, my mum and my sister. I wasn't guided there; it's just where my subconscious mind wanted to lead me. I had multiple revelations and I shed two tears: one from each eye. It was emotional (and I'm not usually very emotional). And all this was from focusing on, and altering, my breath.

We breathe all day, every day and yet, often, we don't do it properly. When we feel stressed, we might find ourselves shallow breathing, or holding our breath without realizing. The way we breathe affects the oxygen and carbon dioxide balance in our bodies – we need to bring oxygen into our bloodstream and expel carbon dioxide – and so paying attention to our breath can help with the physical body as well as the mind.

"By breathing deeply," reads an article on Deepak Chopra's website, "you can activate your parasympathetic nervous system, and, in turn, slow down your heart rate and lower your blood pressure, creating a feeling of calm. You also rely on your diaphragm instead of your chest, inviting your neck and chest muscles to relax and engage your abs and a larger amount of oxygen to reach your body's cells and organs."[8] It can also help with depression, anxiety and PTSD. The article goes on to describe the "spirit" connection with breathwork: "When you practise, you can move beyond your body and mind, and connect with your core spirit – your Self. In other words, you can remove your ego and connect to your true Self and the Universe. Many people who practice breathwork experience spiritual awakenings or attunements to their inner being."

If you're feeling stressed during the working day, you can take a breathwork break. Go and find somewhere to sit comfortably or lie down and do this exercise that Claire Frances shared with me. It only takes five minutes.

Breath awareness by Claire Frances

Sit in a meditation pose, or lie down. Set a timer for one minute.

Watch your breath coming in through the nose, then out through the nose. Pay attention to the texture of your

---

[8]   "How Breathwork Benefits the Mind, Body, and Spirit", chopra.com, 5 October 2020

breath, how it feels in your nostrils and where it lands in your body. Is it going into your chest, your belly?

When we feel anxious or stressed, we might do shallow breathing. You don't need to go into your head and question why, just observe. You're checking in with yourself to see where you're at, in that moment.

Let's do a heart coherence breath: breathe in for five counts, then out for five. Again, inhale and exhale through the nose. You are breathing into the heart space, so you might like to put your hand on your heart while you breathe. You want to bring the breath all the way down into your belly, but you're focusing on the breath coming through your heart. This is a way to oxygenate the body and come into a state of calm. And it activates the parasympathetic nervous system – rest and digest – so it helps us to really slow things down. Especially if, from the "breath awareness", you've noticed that your breath is quite shallow.

Do this for five minutes, every day, for seven days.

2

DESIGN YOUR DREAM LIFE
(IN SEVEN DAYS)

"I think different religions are different doors to the same house. Sometimes I think the house exists, and sometimes I don't. It's the great mystery." Steve Jobs

When I was 24, I finished my journalism masters degree in London, packed my boxes into my car and went to live with my then-boyfriend in Somerset, in southwest England. I had a romantic idea about shacking up with him in a cottage, keeping chickens and reading the papers by a roaring log fire. All of that happened; it was a truly romantic chapter of my life . . . but something else happened, too. Well, two things.

First, I found myself scrambling around for work, as journalism opportunities in the West Country were rather sparse, particularly at that time, with online journalism only in its early stages. Most jobs were in print journalism (and in London). I interned at the *Western Gazette* regional newspaper for a few months, before the job I was aiming to get was taken by some guy from London. I was annoyed. He was confused. And now I was spending long days at the cottage – with only chickens for company – and looking at a rather depressing bank balance.

However, the second thing that happened was I'd recently read Rhonda Byrne's book *The Secret*, which is all about the law of attraction. The theory of it is that what you focus on, you attract into your life. So if you spend all your time feeling really angry with your neighbours, for instance, you will attract more disputes with the local community. It makes sense, when you think about it, because harbouring all that negative energy will affect your interactions with people. If you speak negatively about others and spread hate, it will likely lead to more of the same.

But, equally, if you spend time focusing on how grateful you are for – let's say – your new client and the money they are bringing in, you'll attract more great clients and earn more and more money. That positive, excited energy that you will be emanating, as you experience gratitude – rather than resentment or anger – will enliven you. It will attract people to you, because a person with a big, wide smile and twinkling eyes is infinitely more appealing than someone standing in the corner grimacing.

So that's the basic premise of the law of attraction. Some people talk about universal energies and say that what you put out in the world, you get back: there is a "god" looking over you and delivering bounty to the "good" people and leaving the "bad" people lacking.

I prefer to see the law of attraction as a form of positive psychology, in which focusing on the good in your life and reaching for more joy and positivity helps you to feel better in body, mind and spirit, so you see new opportunities, make more connections with people and live a bigger, fuller and more fulfilling life.

During that slightly low period at the cottage, I returned to *The Secret* and re-read it. I knew that I needed to focus on what I did want, rather than wondering: Why didn't I get that job? Why is it so hard to become a freelance journalist? Why am I working so hard and yet not succeeding? Why am I not earning enough money?

I pulled out a piece of A4 paper and wrote "Annie's Aims" at the top. I listed five things I would like to be doing or achieving and I wrote them – as instructed in *The Secret* – in the present tense. The idea of that is to feel as though your list is already happening and so it becomes your reality sooner, because if you believe it is happening – or close to happening – you are more open to opportunities that will lead you towards your goal or dream.

My five aims were:

- To become a successful freelance journalist.
- To have a book published.
- To make music and perform it to thousands.
- To perform my poetry in front of thousands.
- To spread love around the world.

I tacked it up on the wall and forgot all about it. Once, a relative was visiting and I caught him smiling as he read my list. I was a bit embarrassed at first. I thought he might make fun of me. To me, it wasn't an unusual thing to do – write out my dreams – but I knew that not everyone is raised to dream and believe and work towards an even better future. I was wrong, though. He said: "I love this list, especially the bit about spreading love."

Fast forward ten years (yeah, it didn't happen overnight) and I'd written, as a journalist, for national newspapers, glossy magazines and more. I'd spoken on BBC radio and done panel talks alongside celebrities, speaking in front of hundreds of people. I'd had one book published, another was just coming out and I'd started working on my third book proposal (for this book, actually). I'd written poetry that had gone viral on Instagram after being shared by the musician Paloma Faith and the Hollywood star and activist Busy Philipps. And, while I wasn't doing live performances of my poetry, I was sharing videos of it online that reached thousands of people, likewise my music compositions.

As to whether or not I had succeeded in spreading love around the world . . . well, that's harder to measure. But you know what? I'm wondering if this book – and the work I'm doing on raising awareness of spiritual intelligence – might just be how I start to spread more love.

Anyway, reflecting on those aims, it became clear to me that when you really know what you want and you stay focused on it and work hard, it can absolutely all happen. Back then, in that cottage in Somerset with my four chickens, I had no idea that I'd go on to have the career I've had so far. My aims felt ludicrous, like the wildest dreams. But I was – and remain – a dreamer and if you dare to dream, and then to act, well, magical things can happen.

As I moved through the next decade, I'd had two children and my third was on his way. I'd been working hard to build a freelance career that I could continue while mothering, but I was only earning around £2,000 a month and felt like I was just scraping by; there wasn't any surplus. I wanted to earn really good money, but not at the expense of time with my children, so I created a new set of dreams, including earning £100,000 in a year, living in the countryside (again) and working just a few hours a day.

Again, I noted this down in a notebook and then moved on with my life. Continuing to work hard on my career, continuing to spend time with my children, but not fixating on my new list. And then, in the spring of 2019, I launched an online course. My first book, *The Freelance Mum*, was all about setting up as a freelancer after having a baby. My readers told me that they wanted more tips for getting press coverage, so I created a course called "DIY PR", teaching women how to secure really good coverage. I launched that course and ten women signed up, paying £300 each. That was an extra £3,000 that month, bringing my income up to £5,000. I couldn't believe it. I relaunched the same course the next month and this time 30 women signed up (£9,000). I created a second course, then a third. Soon, I was running an online course business.

As I approached the birth of my third baby, my husband quit his job to help me run my business. This meant that we could truly share the home and business workload, without having to always take it in turns to work. I have fond memories of those early months: pushing the buggy to the coffee shop for a work meeting with my husband, coming up with creative marketing ideas, home for some work on the laptop while rocking the baby in his bouncer. My husband would make delicious lunches, because he had the time. And then we'd collect our older two children from school together and finish our working day. Soon, we were bringing in £10,000 a month from our courses, which increased to £20,000 a month during the pandemic.

I'd been clear on my dream and it had materialized. Not in the way I'd imagined – I'd never even considered working with my husband – but it doesn't always matter how a dream manifests, as long as it does. And throughout those first few years of running my business, I was reciting magic spells, calling on deities such as Vesta – goddess of home, hearth and harmony – to guide me, as well as carrying special gemstones with me wherever I went. I'll share more details about all of that in the coming chapters, but the starting point is getting clear on what it is that you want.

I was also doing deep visualizations around attracting customers for my courses. I'd close my eyes and visualize a sea of lovely, gentle, kind and ambitious women in front of me. I'd imagine a warm, glowing light emanating from my heart and stretching towards each individual woman's heart, connecting us. The more I imagined these women, the more wonderful women signed up. You see, these visualizations – and getting clear on who I wanted to attract – helped me to create the right messaging for social media. And the women with whom my message resonated were the ones who signed up. I now have an online community of several thousand women and the email conversations we have are golden. We support and encourage each other, share words of wisdom and offer each other work opportunities. This, for me, is the magical side of manifesting.

You have to keep your wits about you, though. Be wary of those who are selling "manifesting" as the instant, quick-and-easy answer to all your woes. There are businesses that promise something they can't deliver: definite results, and they are preying on vulnerable people (often women). With manifesting, you can't ever be sure of the outcome, because *you* have to do the work. You can't set an intention, send it off into the ether and think that it will magically land on your doorstep. It won't. You have to continue to work towards your dream or goal. If you add a splash of SQ, it will be all the more powerful. More on that in a minute.

First, here is an example of how manifesting works. Let's say you want a new car. If you get clear on the car you'd love – the brand, design, colour, cost – you can then start doing the necessary work towards getting that car. That might mean saving up, allocating existing savings or borrowing money. Eventually, you'll be able to get that car.

But there are two issues with the mainstream manifesting conversation. One is that it is a whole lot easier to "manifest" something related to wealth if you come from a wealthy family. For instance, that car might actually just arrive outside your house if your mum earns hundreds of thousands of pounds a year and loves giving you surprise gifts. Most of us don't have this luxury, but for those who do, they are not "manifesting" in the spiritual sense, they are just the beneficiary of great wealth.

The other misconception is that you set the intention, click your fingers and – wham bam strawberry jam – your new BMW is parked in the driveway. Or, worse, you get yourself into huge debt buying a car that you can't afford right now because you've been told that, if you want it, you can have it. So there is an element of responsibility that we each need to take when manifesting. Look at your dreams, look at where you're at and look at a reasonable timeline within which your goals might happen. Remember, all those aims I mentioned earlier took ten years to come to fruition.

In support of manifesting is the simple fact that, if you don't know that you want that car, you won't get it. So, shall we move on to what it *is* that you want? And remember: I said that, to start, we'll do some more general life-coaching exercises and mindset work before moving on to the SQ. One step at a time.

YOUR SEVEN-DAY "DREAM LIFE" PLAN

Designing your dream life should be fun. It involves, of course, dreaming . . . but perhaps in ways you haven't dreamed before. I will provide the coaching exercises and prompts that you need to get really clear on what a wonderful present and future looks like for you, and I'd recommend that you work through them over the course of seven days. It works well to commit to a specific time when you will do the day's exercises (first thing in the morning, when you sit at your work desk, lunchtime, after dinner, just before bed and so on). Set aside half an hour, make sure you have a notepad and pen to hand and find somewhere calm and quiet where you won't be disturbed. After the seven days, you should be feeling clearer, more focused and excited about where you're headed, in terms of both your home and work life.

Here's what you'll be focusing on each day . . .

- Day 1. Bird's-eye view (taking a zoomed-out look at your life).
- Day 2. Core values (what really matters to you).
- Day 3. Your SQ wish list (everything you want).
- Day 4. Comfort zone (how to live within it, as well as stretching it).
- Day 5. Gratitude (noticing what you already have).
- Day 6. Vision-boarding (a visual representation of your dream life).
- Day 7. Manifesto (one for the wall).

When you're ready to get started, here's the exercise for Day 1 . . .

Day 1. Bird's-eye view

To start, I'd like you to take a zoomed-out look at your life. We spend so much time consumed with the minor everyday stuff – chores, looking after others, earning money, friendships and so on – and sometimes it can be really beneficial to zoom right out and just look at everything that we have going on. So when you have thoughts such as: *I'm barely doing anything, but for some reason, I'm exhausted.* Or: *I really want to do this new thing but I can't seem to find the time (or energy)*, you might start to understand why. It's because you are probably doing a lot of things, all the time. And so it can help to get clear on just how much you have going on right now.

As a coach, it's important to me that you approach life-planning from a grounded position. While the idea of scrapping all the messy parts of life and diving right into the life of our dreams is so appealing (for me: sitting on a Caribbean beach most days, heading to a quiet writer's hut to pen my next book, pulling fresh fruit from a nearby tree . . .) we need to look at what our life is actually like right now. From there, we can identify what's working – what we want to keep – as well as what we can drop. And then we can start to create space for the beautiful dreams we have for the future. So let's start with where you are at, in your life, right now.

Get yourself a sheet of A4 and write your name in the middle. Now draw a circle around it. (See the diagram overleaf as an example of how this might look.) Remember, this exercise is all about *you*. You are in the centre of the piece of paper, signifying that you are the centre of your own life.

Once you've done that, I'd like you to draw little lines going off your circle and, at the top of each, name one thing you have going on in your life right now that matters. These shouldn't be responsibilities, or obligations from the past, or stuff that's

Bird's-eye View
With examples

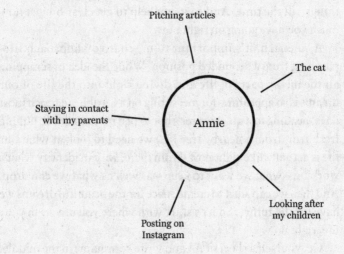

Pitching articles

The cat

Staying in contact
with my parents

Annie

Looking after
my children

Posting on
Instagram

planned for the future, just all that you have going on in the present. This list might be quite long and that's fine; get everything down.

If you'd like some prompts, you could think about:

- Community
- Creativity
- Family
- Friends
- Health and fitness
- Hobbies
- Home
- Nature
- Paid work
- Pets
- Voluntary work

Once you've done this, I'd like you to circle the three areas that are most important to you.

And, after that, can you narrow it down to one?

And remember: this exercise is about *you*. Not what someone else thinks you should prioritize but what *you* would like to prioritize.

You will come up with your own ideas, but to give an example, right now I am prioritizing work and earning. It doesn't mean that my kids don't matter to me, or that I have no time for friends, but it means I want to focus the majority of my energy and attention on work. A year ago, I relocated from the city to the countryside and, during that time, I was focusing a lot of time and attention on helping my family to settle into our new home and schools. Now that we've settled, I'm hungry for work and earning and creating and innovating.

Once you've given some time and thought to this exercise,

I'd like you to look at both your top three, and your top one, priority.

You've looked at what's most important to you and what you'd like to prioritize. Now here are some questions to ponder: you can think about them, chat about them with someone else, or put pen to paper . . .

- Where does your top one feature in your life? How close are you to prioritizing it?
- If your top priority is not getting the time or effort you'd like, how could you shift the balance?
- What's one step you could take today to start that shift happening?
- How do you feel, having identified this area?
- Is there anything that isn't serving you, that you can let go of?
- If so, when will you stop doing it?
- How will you feel, once it's no longer in your life?
- What will you use that time for instead?
- How do you feel, having spent some time thinking about yourself and your life?

SQ EXPERIENCE: FREE MOVEMENT

I was nearing the end of my working day and felt as if my body had stiffened up, so I did what I do most days: put on a playlist of world music, lay on the floor of my (quite small) office and started to breathe in time to the music. In, out, in, out. The conscious connected breathwork that Claire Frances taught me. As I started to breathe heavily – and then fast – I felt as if I wanted to move my body, so I began to move into yoga positions such as downward dog and child's pose, before creating my own poses. I stretched my legs and arms and neck and feet, pointing, twisting, pushing. It felt heavenly, to move and stretch in this way.

After around 20 minutes, I turned off the music – my body still tingling – noted down some thoughts I'd had and got on with my day. When I told my husband about how good it had felt to roll around my office doing breathwork to music, he said: "Imagine if the roofers had seen you do that?" (We were having building work done that day.) *What if they had?* I thought. They might have laughed or been bemused, but they might have also thought: *That looks good, I'd like to try that.* So I wanted to share some simple instructions for giving it a go yourself.

Some people refer to this practice as "ecstatic dance" and others as "non-linear movement". But both mean something similar: moving your body in a way that feels good, to music, with no rules or restrictions. You can shake your body, stretch it, bounce, just lie still, bring in your knees while you lie on your back, be on all fours. Whatever you fancy, at exactly the pace that feels right for you. As ever, listen to your body, don't do anything that hurts and – if you are pregnant or suffering with an injury – check with your doctor first.

- Find somewhere you can be alone for 15–20 minutes.
- Bring your phone and search for a "breathwork" playlist on Spotify or YouTube.
- Start by lying on your back, on the floor.
- Focus on your breathing: in and out, in time to the music. Start by breathing through your nose, then try both inhaling and exhaling through your mouth.
- You might like to start experimenting with your breath: faster inhalations and exhalations, or holding on the out breath.
- When you feel ready, start to move your body, with your eyes closed.
- You could stretch out an arm or leg, bring it back in, roll over, go on all fours, stand up and squat, lift your leg, go on tiptoes, reach for the sky, flop over like a rag doll, bounce up and down, shake your bottom. Whatever feels good.
- Keep going for as long as you like. You can set an alarm if you need to be somewhere at a specific time.
- Remember: no one is watching. And even if they are: who cares?
- Notice how you feel in your body, now.

Day 2. Core values

When I first did a "values" exercise – about five years ago – I'd never thought about what mattered to me, in this way. At the time, I was doing client work and chose my clients according to whether they paid me enough and whether they weren't completely unreasonable. (Though some of them were . . . and I still worked for them, as I needed the money.)

Before that, when I was studying for my masters degree in journalism, I remember my tutor teaching that it was really important to be clear on who you want to be, morally, as a journalist, before you set out. Of course, all journalism is about telling an honest story about a real-life person or event, but some journalists are open to less orthodox – or morally questionable – methods for drawing out a story. So what my tutor was really saying was: get clear on your values before you set out and try to stick to them. In time, this really made sense to me. I've sometimes tripped up and gone against my values or instinct, but, on the whole, I am true to what I believe is right. So although I hadn't done a formal values exercise, I'd been inadvertently considering my values and (largely) enforcing them in my work.

But now, over to *you* and your values.

You may have done values exercises before, you may not. Either is fine. If you have, it's worth repeating the exercise quite regularly, as your values may change over time. As our lives shift and change, sometimes the things that matter most to us do, too. Also, you might find that your values stay the same, but you are no longer honouring them.

So, for this exercise, I've put together a list of over 450 values (see pages 43–5, or you can also download lists of values online). These are words about ways of being and behaving. It's worth reading – well, skimming – through all these words and seeing which jump out at you. Which make you think: *Yes , that matters so much to me.* Or: *I'd like to be more like that.* Every time you see one of those words, write it down. Note as many as you like that matter to you. Your list may be long or short. Either is fine. We're all different, we have varying experiences and we're all at different places on this journey of life.

Above and beyond
Acceptance
Accessibility
Accomplishment
Accountability
Accuracy
Achievement
Activity
Adaptability
Adventure
Adventurous
Affection
Affective
Agility
Aggressiveness
Alertness
Altruism
Ambition
Amusement
Anti-bureaucratic
Anticipation
Anti-corporate
Appreciation
Approachability
Assertiveness
Attention to detail
Attentiveness
Availability
Awareness
Balance
Beauty
Being the best
Belonging
Best
Best people
Bold
Boldness
Bravery
Brilliance
Calm
Calmness
Candour
Capability
Carefulness
Caring
Certainty
Challenge

Change
Character
Charity
Cheerful
Citizenship
Cleanliness
Clear
Clear-minded
Clever
Clients
Collaboration
Comfort
Commitment
Common sense
Communication
Community
Compassion
Competence
Competency
Competition
Competitive
Completion
Composure
Comprehensive
Concentration
Concern for others
Confidence
Confidentiality
Conformity
Connection
Consciousness
Consistency
Contentment
Continuity
Continuous improvement
Contribution
Control
Conviction
Cooperation
Coordination
Cordiality
Correct
Courage
Courtesy
Craftiness
Craftsmanship
Creation

Creativity
Credibility
Cunning
Curiosity
Customer focus
Customer satisfaction
Customer service
Daring
Decency
Decisive
Decisiveness
Dedication
Delight
Democratic
Dependability
Depth
Determination
Determined
Development
Devotion
Devout
Different
Differentiation
Dignity
Diligence
Directness
Discipline
Discovery
Discretion
Dominance
Down-to-earth
Dreaming
Drive
Duty
Eagerness
Ease of use
Economy
Education
Effectiveness
Efficiency
Elegance
Empathy
Employees
Empowering
Encouragement
Endurance
Energy
Engagement

Enjoyment
Entertainment
Enthusiasm
Entrepreneurship
Environment
Equality
Ethical
Exceed expectations
Excellence
Excitement
Exhilarating
Experience
Expertise
Exploration
Expressive
Extrovert
Exuberance
Fairness
Faith
Faithfulness
Family
Family atmosphere
Famous
Fashion
Fast
Fearless
Ferocious
Fidelity
Fierce
Firm
Fitness
Flair
Flexibility
Fluency
Focus
Focus on future
Foresight
Formal
Fortitude
Freedom
Fresh
Fresh ideas
Friendly
Friendship
Frugality
Fun
Generosity

Genius
Giving
Global
Goodness
Goodwill
Gratitude
Greatness
Growth
Guidance
Happiness
Hard work
Harmony
Health
Heart
Helpful
Heroism
History
Holiness
Honesty
Honour
Hope
Hospitality
Humble
Humility
Humour
Hygiene
Imagination
Impact
Impartial
Impious
Improvement
Independence
Individuality
Industry
Informal
Innovative
Inquisitive
Insightful
Inspiration
Integrity
Intelligence
Intensity
International
Intuitive
Invention
Investment
Inviting
Irreverence
Joy

Justice
Kindness
Knowledge
Leadership
Learning
Legal
Level-headed
Liberty
Listening
Lively
Local
Logic
Longevity
Love
Loyalty
Mastery
Maturity
Maximizing
Maximum
    utilization
Meaning
Meekness
Mellow
Members
Meritocracy
Meticulous
Mindful
Moderation
Modesty
Motivation
Mystery
Neatness
Nerve
No bureaucracy
Obedience
Open-minded
Openness
Optimism
Order
Organization
Originality
Outrageous
Partnership
Passion
Patience
Patient-centered
Patient-focused
Patient-
    satisfaction

Patriotism
Peace
People
Perception
Perceptive
Perfection
Performance
Perseverance
Persistence
Personal
    development
Personal growth
Persuasive
Philanthropy
Play
Playfulness
Pleasantness
Poise
Polish
Popularity
Positive
Potency
Potential
Powerful
Practical
Pragmatic
Precision
Prepared
Preservation
Pride
Privacy
Proactive
Productivity
Profane
Professionalism
Profitability
Profits
Progress
Prosperity
Prudence
Punctuality
Purity
Pursuit
Quality
Quality of work
Rational
Real
Realistic
Reason

Recognition
Recreation
Refined
Reflection
Relationships
Relaxation
Reliability
Reliable
Resilience
Resolute
Resolution
Resourcefulness
Respect
Respect for
    others
Respect for the
    individual
Responsibility
Responsiveness
Rest
Restraint
Results-oriented
Reverence
Rigor
Risk taking
Rule of law
Sacrifice
Safety
Sanitary
Satisfaction
Security
Self-control
Self-directed
Self-motivation
Self-
    responsibility
Selfless
Self-reliance
Sense of
    humour
Sensitivity
Serenity
Serious
Service
Shared
    prosperity
Sharing
Shrewd
Significance

DESIGN YOUR DREAM LIFE (IN SEVEN DAYS)

Silence
Silliness
Simplicity
Sincerity
Skill
Skillfulness
Smart
Solitude
Speed
Spirit
Spirituality
Spontaneous
Stability
Standardization
Status
Stealth
Stewardship
Strength

Structure
Success
Support
Surprise
Sustainability
Sympathy
Synergy
Systemization
Talent
Teamwork
Temperance
Thankful
Thorough
Thoughtful
Timeliness
Timely
Tolerance
Toughness

Traditional
Training
Tranquility
Transparent
Trustworthy
Truth
Understanding
Unflappability
Uniqueness
Unity
Universal
Useful
Utility
Valour
Value
Value
  creation
Variety

Victorious
Vigor
Virtue
Vision
Vitality
Warmth
Watchfulness
Wealth
Welcoming
Willfulness
Winning
Wisdom
Wonder
Worldwide
Work-life
  balance

Once you have your list of all the values that resonated, see if you can narrow it down to your top three. Now, look at those three values.

How are you living them, if you are? In what ways are you honouring these values?

I'll give you an example. One of my top values is "comfort". I like taking risks, so this word does not signify a comfort zone, but more physical comfort – such as my clothes – and boundaries. I will take a risk in business, but I will not – whenever possible (we all trip up occasionally) – let people push me into doing something that just isn't right, for me or someone I care for. In terms of comfort with clothes, I don't wear belts, ever, or dangly jewellery that might catch. I don't wear tight jeans or any clothes that feel "fussy". And I prioritize really soft bedsheets, an amazing memory foam pillow and a calm bedroom.

In business, comfort might relate to pricing and never charging more than I think a product or service is worth. Or that I'd pay. So that's one of my values – probably the top one – and some ways that I honour it.

A lovely thing happened recently. My daughter, who's eight, told me that she and her new friend were discussing clothing. Her friend said: "My mum likes me to wear fashionable clothes." And my daughter said: "Well, my mum focuses more on comfort." I loved hearing how something that matters so much to me is filtering down to my daughter. It matters to me that she is comfortable at home and school and wears clothes that she can run and jump about in.

Another of my core values is "freedom"; that one was tested pretty hard during the pandemic. But I still found ways to feel free, even while contained. I would go for a run in the morning, I would read a novel before bed so that I could escape in my mind. I would stand in the garden, alone, looking up at the sky (see page 87 for more on Skychology). More recently, I bought myself a car, because sharing one with my husband meant I would have to check with him before using it. Now, I can jump in my car and whizz off to the swimming pool, or to London, or wherever I like.

Sometimes it's really easy to see what we need to do in order to honour our values and be true to ourselves, while at other times we have to think a little creatively about how to honour them. So here are some questions about your values for you to ponder:

- How are you honouring your top three values?
- If you're not, why not? What's getting in the way?
- Could you work to remove that barrier?
- What parts of your life do these values impact?
- How could you work your values into your home and working life even more?
- How would it feel, if you did that?
- What one change can you make, today, to honour your values even more?

Now, I'd like you to think back to the bird's-eye view exercise (see page 35) and the area you chose that you'd like to prioritize:

- How does this fit with your values?
- When you give your time to that one area, are you also honouring your values more?

Okay, let's get going with the SQ twist.

Do you know what's amazing about connecting with something bigger than ourselves? Opening up to the idea of magic? Deciding that, while we can have our feet placed firmly on the ground, we can also let our mind wander up into the clouds and beyond? Well, it's that it means there are no limits to what we can do, see, be and achieve.

When we break free from the idea that only some people can

do certain things and others can't, our dreams become bigger. "Bigger," by the way, doesn't need to be linked to anything financial. It could be about finding more time for yourself, or for friends. It could be about a different work-life balance. It could be about a hobby or a new business you'd like to start. A pet you'd like to have. Whatever it is, it's about doing it for *you*. Because it's okay to have dreams for yourself. They might impact other people, but, right now, we are focusing on what *you* want.

As an example, perhaps you want to live abroad for a while. And your partner or children or parents don't want that for you (or themselves). If that is your dream, then that has a place in your SQ wish list and your vision board (see pages 51 and 80). We spend a lot of time thinking about what others need from us and creating limitations about what is and isn't possible for ourselves, because of how it would affect those other people. But I invite you to ignore everyone else during these exercises and focus inward.

Now, we are going to do a coaching exercise to help you start to work out what it is that you want. What your dream life looks like. I would love it if you could approach this exercise in what we might describe as an "embodied way". That means: while you are imagining this future life in your head, you are also feeling it in your body, as if you are already there. You might like to imagine that you're surrounded by a glowing golden light, or another visual that feels really magical and ethereal: an aura, if you like. I want you to feel magical and glowing as you work through the following exercises. This is the "spirit" link.

Look ahead to this time next year.

What would your life look like if you were living fully by your values and prioritizing the area you identified?

You might like to close your eyes and really visualize you, next year, living your best life. Feel your way into it. Breathe deeply, in through your nose, out through your mouth. Relax, imagine, dream:

- You could think about where you're living, what work you're doing (this might include – or be – a caring role).
- What you're eating, what you're wearing.
- What your day-to-day looks like in the week, then at the weekends.
- Do you have holidays?
- And hobbies, do you have any? What are they?
- What do you look like?
- Who are you surrounded by?
- How does it feel, imagining a life where you're being true to – and living out – your values?

Now, you are hopefully clearer on what's going on in your life right now, so tomorrow we can go in deeper on your vision.

And remember, your values may change over time, so this is an exercise you can keep coming back to whenever you're feeling a bit lost or confused.

SQ in the world
Writers on SQ

As a writer, I know the feeling of an idea "dropping in" from somewhere unknown. Here, other writers share the ways SQ plays a part in their writing process.

"The world is full of magic things, patiently waiting for our senses to grow sharper."

WB Yeats

"You do not need to work to become spiritual. You are spiritual; you need only to remember that fact. Spirit is within you."

Julia Cameron

"From what we are, spirit; from what we do, matter. Matter and spirit are one."

Philip Pullman

"Re-examine all you have been told. Dismiss what insults your soul."

Walt Whitman

"The soul is placed in the body like a rough diamond, and must be polished, or the lustre of it will never appear."

Daniel Defoe

"When a man is willing and eager, the gods join in."

Aeschylus

"The aim of life is to live, and to live means to be aware; joyously, drunkenly, serenely, divinely aware."

Henry Miller

Day 3. Your SQ wish list

As a child, I loved Christmas, as I expect most children who celebrate it do. It's a time to come together, celebrate and – of course – give and receive gifts. But what makes it all the more magical is the idea that there's a guy called Father Christmas who has a huge toy-making factory in the snowy North Pole, run by elves. While picturing this magical place, children gather by the fireside and write letters to Father Christmas, or Santa, greeting him and listing everything they would like. It doesn't really matter how many of the gifts children actually receive from their list, a large part of the fun is in just sitting there and dreaming about all those shiny new toys you'd like.

At some stage, as we move from child to adolescent, the truth about Father Christmas comes crashing in and (at least temporarily) ruins this part of the year for us. *He isn't real*, an older kid will tell us . . . and we'll have to decide whether they are telling the truth or not. But, by then, we'll probably have spent some time trying to catch him delivering the presents on his sleigh and maybe spotting Mum drinking the sherry left out for him, or Dad eating the mince pie. So the match has been lit for the truth bomb that Father Christmas is, in fact, your mum, dad or carer. And at that point, the *magic* of writing a list dissipates. Instead, it becomes a shopping list that the teenage-you presents to your parent or carer late in the year, expecting them to go and buy things for you.

But what if we decided to return to the magical list-writing, in front of a roaring fire? Because, really, this is the basis of manifesting, the law of attraction and spiritual visualization. The idea that, when you are really clear on exactly what it is that you want, eventually the Universe will deliver it, just like Father Christmas used to. Yes, he isn't "real", but guess what? You are a version of Father Christmas, too. You can be both the hopeful child and the wonderful deliverer of gifts. You can make the list and deliver the bounty (to yourself). All you need is a drove of elves to help you. Magical, invisible helpers.

So now it's time to write your SQ wish list, that is, everything that you want. But I'd like you to return to how it felt to be the child you once were, as you wrote out all the presents you were hoping to receive that year. If you didn't celebrate Christmas, perhaps you can channel the belief you had in the Tooth Fairy, or another magical invented character. Fairies at the bottom of the garden, perhaps, or a deity watching over you, taking note of wishes you made while blowing out the candles on your birthday cake.

Close your eyes and allow yourself to be transported back to childhood, a time – for many of us – when magic and hope and belief were actively encouraged and we didn't question them. Where the excitement of a visit from Father Christmas, or the Tooth Fairy, filled us with a physical buzz, because in that moment we were special. The chosen ones. Now, imagine you are still that chosen child – the special kid whose wishes always come true – and start noting down everything you want. Create an SQ wish list of everything, big and small, that you would like in your life.

You might like to think about:

- Relationships
- Work
- Money
- Emotions
- Place
- Work-life balance
- Food
- Clothing
- Weather
- Health and fitness
- Hobbies

- Time outdoors
- Alone, or surrounded by people
- The noise you'd like to hear

. . . absolutely anything that you *want*.

List as many things as you can. And remember to hold in your body and mind that sensation you had as a child, as you focused on what you wanted and relinquished all responsibility for making it happen, allowing Father Christmas/the Tooth Fairy or whoever to do all the hard work. Feel your way into that unbridled excitement, the giddiness of really believing that these things might just be arriving on your pillow – or doorstep – very soon.

As you get clearer on what you want on your SQ wish list, you might just start to notice some of those things "magically" appearing in your life. Are they magically appearing, or is it that you have opened your mind to them appearing and so you're looking in new, innovative places for them? Remember, the more you focus on the things you don't want, the more you notice them (for instance: angry drivers, people skipping the supermarket queue, people leaving you out of social events). But the more you focus on the beautiful things that you do want in your life, the more you will welcome in.

Soon, you will be spotting an opportunity to make that meal you love, or have it cooked for you. Creating space in your day for time with a particular person, or alone, doing an activity you love. Squirrelling away some of your savings to invest in a product for yourself or the home that you've had your eye on for ages.

Here are some examples of things that I have put on my SQ wish list that have then come true.

I love spaghetti carbonara. My kids don't like it, but I do. So I put it on my list and being clear that I like this, even if no one else around me does, made me feel inspired to cook it. I bought the best Parmesan, the finest lardons, organic eggs and fresh pasta.

And as I stood in the kitchen, whipping up that carbonara, sipping a glass of crisp white wine, I felt joyful. I was doing something for me; cooking a dish that I was going to really enjoy. When I served it, no one else ate much of it, but that didn't (really) matter: I enjoyed it.

Generally, I'm not that into cooking. I do, however, love being cooked for. But it used to rarely happen, because I had become the person in our home who did the food shopping, thought of what to cook and stood at the stove in the early evening, making something for our family to eat. However, once I'd really thought through the fact that I don't like cooking that much and do love being cooked for, I chatted to my husband about it. Turns out, he's happy to cook. So now, often, he does. And I feel grateful, as it's such a treat when he cooks but it feels like a chore when I do.

I have also, in the past, written many other things on my list, including: I want to live in a place where I'm surrounded by nature, I want a slower and quieter life. Compared to the carbonara dream, these are longer-term goals – "bigger" ones, if you like – but I now do live on the edge of countryside and have a slower and quieter life. Actually, it's not that quiet, as I have three young children who run around the house jumping on the sofas and shouting as they pretend to be superheroes, but I can leave them with their dad and head off into the woods for a 20-minute solo walk, listening to the birds, watching the river flow past, dipping my toes in the water and focusing on my breath.

Until I had thought about what I wanted to eat for dinner (spaghetti carbonara), I was eating what everyone else wanted every day. Until I had thought about the fact that I wanted someone else to cook for me, I was doing all the cooking. I'd love a private chef, but that's not going to happen. Financially, it's not where we're at. (And even if it was, I'm not sure I'd want someone in my house every day.) Who knows, perhaps in the future things will change. But, in the meantime, I just became clear on the simple fact that I don't want to cook . . . and my husband heard this. My sister did too. She loves cooking and so, when she came to stay with her sons recently, she cooked for us on both nights. It was so, so lovely. For her, it's a joy. She's happy to potter away in the kitchen, experimenting with different flavours and textures, while I'm happy to watch the kids.

Knowing what you want – and sharing this with other people – makes it more likely to happen.

One last thing I put on my list:

I mentioned that "comfort" is one of my top values and I really wanted some new clothes that reflected this. So I visualized myself drifting through life in lovely light-coloured linen clothes. Soon after writing the list, I launched a course that went well enough that I could invest in new clothes. I went online shopping and bought some lovely, flowing, comfortable clothes. I really don't like shopping, but I do like nice clothes. So getting clear on how I wanted to feel in the clothes lodged the idea in my mind that I would soon own garments like this, which gave me the impetus to launch the course, make it successful and then feel justified in investing in new clothes.

Once you've written out your SQ wish list, I have some questions for you:

- Can you make one of those things happen today?
- Which one?
- When are you going to do it?
- Get clear on your timings and *commit*.
- Is there anyone you can speak to – by email, phone, or in person – who can help you to get one of the things from your list?
- How will you feel, once everything on your list is ticked off?
- How do you feel now, about the idea of having everything that you want?

MY SQ JOURNEY

Rebecca Ferguson, executive producer for television and film.

Spirituality came later for me. I'd say it started in my twenties, on a yoga mat, as often these things do, and I experienced that sense of peace. I started to see how my life was changing with that regular practice and how that informed how I went into the world. I would say my mother and her lineage are very spiritual and intuitive. My paternal line was Catholic and my lovely Nanny's life was entirely informed by Catholicism. She was devout. Organized religion was a great comfort to her. I struggle with some of the central tenets of Catholicism and so does my dad, but it was important to Nanny and we respected that.

I discovered TM, transcendental meditation, when I was 32. I went every Tuesday night to class in Victoria in London and we went into collective group meditation for two hours. Initially the benefits were mostly deep relaxation, but the deeper the practice became, the more synchronicities would start showing up in my life. I started to relish that conversation and found huge comfort in it. Through deepening that practice, I developed a real understanding that we are energetic beings having a human experience and it gave me a perspective that was very welcome when dealing with life's challenges. And the deeper you go down the rabbit hole, the more you realize how much of a dialogue it is. It's not just about receiving some stress relief, you're in a reciprocal dialogue with "something" – God, Source, the Universe – however you choose to name it, and if you pay attention, it's pure magic.

From a regular meditation practice, I realized I was feeling intuitive pings and began following my gut or ideas more readily to see where they would take me; such as the feeling that I needed to call a certain person and that person would then call – those wonderful synchronicities of life. They were showing up more and more and I was recognizing them in advance. And that's where the "space–time" element became really interesting to me. The more time I spent in deep meditation, the more the ordinary concept of time started to bend. Our group meditations were two and a half hours and often I'd think I'd been under for five minutes, but two hours had flown by.

I'd also have these feelings in business. A "ping" that an idea or person was worth following up. That could be emotional intelligence or intuition, it can be pinned as anything, but it was apparent to me that through the process of TM, my life got better. My relationships got better. My compassion elevated. I still got angry and had normal human emotions, they don't go away just because you discover a spiritual life, but that process led me to something deeper, which was how to tap into intuitive pings and use that energy in all aspects of my life.

The constant dance for me is that I still don't believe in all of it, not 100 per cent. Even when you're in your own practice you might not always believe it or experience a bliss state or benefit at the time. It's often particularly difficult to see the benefit if I'm feeling grouchy or hormonal. But there's always a message, there's always something that happens in those moments.

The more time you spend honing the mind–body connection, the more you learn to rely on your own innate intelligence and are less inclined to rely on power structures or external validation. If I feel pissed off or frustrated by something, I know I can go within and find calm and ground myself. It's a very powerful feeling.

It's during difficult moments that spirituality has become an essential friend. I experienced a particularly tough time just before lockdown and the thing that got me through was being on my yoga mat, sitting in meditation at home and using some of the tools I rely on to ground myself. I was having therapy at that time and I started to realize that talking therapies were somatically reprocessing the trauma in my body rather than releasing it. I'd sit in a chair opposite a lovely therapist, cry, talk, pay a lot of money and leave. I'd feel better for a while and it did help give me an intellectual understanding of what had happened, but it didn't move the pain through my body in the same way that other practices have.

In retrospect, I'm very grateful for that tough time (a lot can change in three years) as it led me to the life I have now and ignited a great new passion: a fascination in science and spirituality, where the biochemical meets the alchemical. This has become a genuine pleasure: reading and learning about the mind–body connection and seeing how you can biochemically put your body into certain states to alter the mind. Wim Hof is a great example of that. It's also led me to work with creatives in a different way through workshops led by the awesome Naomi Lewis, in which movement, meditation and improvisation are used to access creative ideas and ancient technologies used in the original agoras and theatres form the basis of the practices.

Working in the media is very inspiring and creative, it can also be very stressful and challenging. My practices are useful for the highs and lows of my work life. Recently, after a difficult day at work, I did yoga Nidra. I wanted to do a really deep session, so I also did a mini bespoke ritual. I often find movement and breathwork, or automatic writing for subconscious expression, particularly helpful. Repetition of movement (walking a figure of eight) can also regulate the nervous system and open us up to receiving benefits, answers and calming the mind–body. Quick 15-minute practices at the end of the day can have a huge overall impact.

If I can authentically drop into a space of love and compassion, a solution will always appear. And it's often not the solution you think it's going to be. I think the greatest gift from my spiritual practice is elevated compassion (I don't always succeed) and from a place of compassion, I hope loves wins. I assume that everyone is grieving something, and that aggression is the one thing that wrecks my vibe, so I stay clear of that at all costs. Those simple rules coupled with my spiritual practices keep me sane in an increasingly mad world.

SQ rituals

I have personal rituals. I start by asking: what's the tool I need today? And it comes through.

My rituals include:

- *Lighting a candle and fire sipping – a ritual that originated in Ancient Greek times and is where the phrase "fire in the belly" comes from. I sit cross-legged in front of the candle, focus on the flame and then quickly pinch the flame between two fingers and inhale it through one nostril. It helps to clear my mind, or unblock me when I'm feeling stuck.*
- *Movement to music.*
- *Staring into a reflective object for ten minutes or so, until my vision becomes blurry and my nervous system has dropped right down. This is also a way to get into a meditative state.*
- *Automatic writing.*
- *Painting.*
- *Walking a figure of eight. I use sacred geometry a lot: putting my body into a rhythm. So walking a figure of eight is a somatically soothing thing to do. You can get into a deep trance quite quickly.*

- *I find rituals in darkness, at night-time, very soothing. You can light candles or light a fire.*

Working in TV and spirituality

Working in drama is a great pleasure: truly stimulating and inspiring and no day is ever the same. The variety of ideas and people make it a very rewarding career but it can also be highly stressful and demanding. I've mostly been developing and producing drama series for the last five years and, most recently, The Trial of Christine Keeler *and* The Responder *are shows of which I'm very proud.*

I've recently moved to commissioning, which is a different space creatively. You get to work with the entire industry, and I've found great satisfaction in the pivot. I ask myself different questions when reading a script or idea: Will this serve our audience? Who will like to watch this and why? And other times it's entirely instinctual. Sometimes there will be a moment in a meeting or a writer that will give me that true gut reaction of a "YES". It can often take me by surprise when that happens and I love those moments. A writer will just say something that sets your soul ablaze. In that sense, spirituality and creativity are in constant communication in my day to day.

I'm mostly interested in ideas that spark joy and I love the feeling of reading a beautiful script. My work is emotional and spiritual in that regard. "Do I feel the feels?" It's really as simple as that. Has this writer taken me to another space and time? Am I so absorbed in the writer's intention that my cup of tea has gone cold? That's the sign of a great script: it's unputdownable. You don't pick up your phone or check your emails when it's that good. The script allows me into the imagination of the writer, in a sense it's a private moment, like reading a diary. For writers, it's emotional and vulnerable. The act of writing is a spiritual one. The idea of the muse visiting when the writer sits down, bravely, to do the work. My job is to shepherd that to screen and often, when thinking about notes to give or thoughts on an edit, if I'm allowed the space to think and contemplate, I will use meditation for answers rather than constantly being in the thinking–doing mindset.

SQ books I'd recommend

Wild: A journey from lost to found *by Cheryl Strayed*
If Women Rose Rooted: A life-changing journey to authenticity and belonging *by Sharon Blackie*
Becoming Supernatural: How common people are doing the uncommon *by Dr Joe Dispenza*

Day 4. Comfort zone

When I was at university, a friend asked me a question. He asked: "Would you prefer a stable life, or an exciting life?" At the time, I was into partying and travelling, I had different boyfriends and made new friends all over the place. So I said: "Exciting, obviously." I felt that life was for living, not for settling down, or settling for anything other than exciting.

After university, I returned to London and continued living my exciting life: going out a lot, meeting people, taking different courses, doing creative projects. But then I met my husband and I saw that I could enjoy my life with him and that it would be both stable and exciting. Stable because I knew I could trust him: he was kind and respected me. Exciting because I don't believe a marriage or long-term relationship needs to get in the way of you having fun. Both together and on your own.

As I went on to have three children, develop a career, then launch a business, I thought more about the exciting-versus-stable question. Really, it's about living inside or outside your comfort zone.

When you are living fully within your comfort zone, things feel stable. Safe. You might not challenge yourself so much, but neither do you have to deal with the consequences of taking a risk. Sometimes a risk pays off and leads to something amazing, but at other times, it can go disastrously wrong and leave you feeling as if you have failed. Perhaps wishing you hadn't done it at all. Like all things in life, a balance is probably what we ought to strive for.

I sometimes see people who seem to be living entirely within their comfort zone: they have a simple job that they do every day, they have their salary and they know where they stand financially. They spend their weekends pottering around the home and garden, going on small local trips. Maybe they like staycations. Sometimes I think this life looks too small, while at other times I think it looks so easy in a really good way. It's about focusing on the everyday joys, rather than thinking life needs to be filled with big adventures.

But then I'll see someone who travels with their work, who lives in lots of different places, has lots of different creative projects going on and meets people all around the world. And I think: *Yes, this is it. Life is for filling with these types of things.* The flipside to the more exciting life is that there is less stability. Routine is harder to create and perhaps a life of always reaching for more leaves a feeling of dissatisfaction.

But back to the comfort zone.

As you know by now, comfort really matters to me. So operating from within my comfort zone feels good. For that reason, I am very big on my daily routine and I rarely veer from it. I get up at a similar time each day, do my intention-setting, drink three instant coffees while reading a book, get my children their breakfast and then go on a run. I return home for a stretch and shower before I get dressed and take my two older kids to school. I do my pre-work SQ rituals: lighting a candle or scent diffuser, happiness journaling, "dong-ing" my Tibetan singing bowl and pulling a card from my tarot deck. And then work begins, during school hours. I pick my kids up at 3pm and I am on duty for the rest of the evening. I don't often go out on weekday evenings, because it makes me too tired.

Now, to stretch my daily existence outside of my comfort zone might mean going to bed really late and waking up later, but then having to rush in the morning. It might mean going for a swim rather than a run, letting my husband drop the kids at school, working somewhere outside the home. But I've tried all these things and none of them feel as good as my normal habits. So I stick to my comfort zone, which is my daily routine.

However, when it comes to work, I feel very differently. Yes, I have my allotted working hours, which is necessary as I have other responsibilities such as motherhood. But in terms of the work I will do, I'm open to new experiences.

Being a journalist means I have to pitch to editors in order to get a story published. This is pushing myself out of my comfort zone, because I have to convince another person that a particular article is a brilliant idea and that their readers will want to see it. Often, a pitch will be ignored or rejected, so I have to pitch again. Sometimes, I'll re-pitch the same idea three times before it leads to a commission and publication. For a long time, I found it very uncomfortable. However, I just had to do it, as there was no other way. It's a similar process for pitching a book idea to a publisher. You have to believe in yourself enough to keep pushing, even when it feels uncomfortable.

When each of my earlier books, *The Freelance Mum* and *Shy*, were published, I had to do public speaking as part of the publicity drive. Well, I didn't actually *have* to, but I was asked to and I felt a combination of obligation to my publisher and obligation to myself. I felt I owed it to myself to take these opportunities, so that I would grow as a person. I still find public speaking hard, but the more I do it, the more exciting I've started to find it. I think public speaking will always be outside of my comfort zone, I will always feel nervous and, for that reason, I do loads of preparation. But this serves me well, as it means I have well-thought-out answers to any questions I may be asked.

My dad says that we should step out of our comfort zone once a day. After all, stretching, or stepping outside of, our comfort zone leads to growth. But, when we are busy, maybe with young kids or juggling different jobs, it's just another thing to add to the to-do list. So I advocate for regularly testing or stretching your comfort zone, trying things that feel like a bigger challenge, but without putting yourself under unnecessary pressure.

For some of you, the idea of raising your SQ will be outside of your comfort zone. Perhaps you're curious about it, but haven't – until now – delved into how you can create spiritual practices and weave them into your daily life. Or maybe you have, but you haven't told anyone about it for fear that they'll think it's weird. Either way, you are stretching your comfort zone by exploring these new ideas, practices and rituals. So well done.

Now, over to you and your comfort zone:

- I'd like you to name three things you do when you are operating within your comfort zone.
- Now I'd like you to name three things that would take you a little way outside of your comfort zone.
- Now, I would like you to name three things that would seriously challenge your comfort zone. Things that feel kind of wild and perhaps you've never even considered doing before.
- How do you feel about those three things you do that keep you in your comfort zone?
- Do you feel like you want to continue doing things that way?
- Now, how about those three things that push you a little outside of your comfort zone? How often do you do them?
- Would you like to do these things more?
- If yes, what could you do to incorporate them more regularly in your life?
- Would you like to make a commitment to yourself, for when you might do them?
- And what about the final three, the wild ideas that perhaps feel quite out of reach, or unaligned with your current reality? Would you like to do them?
- How would it feel if you went ahead with one of them?
- Would you like to commit to trying it?
- When are you going to do it?
- How does it feel, to be thinking through your comfort zone in this way?

SQ books that inspired Steve Jobs

Steve Jobs, founder of Apple and one of the most innovative tech entrepreneurs the world has ever known, was into spirituality. As a student, he started exploring Buddhism and he continued to practice Zen Buddhism throughout his life. Apparently, Jobs's minimalist approach to design was inspired by his spirituality. He was also deeply influenced by what he'd learned about intuition from Buddhism. "I began to realize that an intuitive understanding and consciousness was more significant than abstract thinking and intellectual logical analysis," he said.[9]

Jobs was heavily influenced by a variety of books on spirituality and enlightenment . . .

Be Here Now by Ram Dass

This is a guide to meditation and the wonders of psychedelic drugs. "It was profound," Jobs said. "It transformed me and many of my friends."

Zen Mind, Beginner's Mind: Informal talks on zen meditation and practice by Shunryū Suzuki

A book of teachings by Shunryū Suzuki, based on talks given in California on the joy and practice of Zen Buddhism.

Autobiography of a Yogi by Paramahansa Yogananda

First published in 1946, Paramahansa Yogananda shares details about his life in this book, his encounters with spiritual figures and how he found his guru. Also he writes about becoming a monk and establishing his teachings of Kriya Yoga meditation. Jobs is said to have read this book once a year throughout his life.

---

[9]   *Steve Jobs*, Walter Isaacson (Little, Brown, 2011)

Cutting Through Spiritual Materialism by Chögyam Trungpa
This book addresses many common pitfalls for those seeking spirituality, which Trungpa coins "spiritual materialism".

Day 5. Gratitude

When my daughter was a toddler, she had wild tantrums. And sometimes, I'd let her thrash it out (safely) because her body just needed to roll around and shake and release some of the pent-up energy. But at other times she wouldn't let that happen and instead she'd tell me, repeatedly, that she wanted a particular thing. Perhaps it was a lollipop in the shop that I didn't want her to have, or a teddy bear. But whatever it was, she wouldn't stop. Until one day, when I came up with a rhyme that made her laugh. As she was going on and on about something she wanted, I turned to her and snapped: "More gratitude, less attitude." We both laughed at this accidental rhyme. And while it didn't solve her tantrums, it did start to make her aware of how much she did have, rather than only focusing on the lack.

In the Dalai Lama's book, *The Art of Happiness*, he writes that: "Happiness is determined more by one's state of mind than by external events." We might experience a burst of excitement if we get a new job, or an opportunity comes our way, but the feeling won't be long-lasting. Soon, we'll return to our baseline of happiness. One way to increase that happiness baseline, though, is to practise gratitude. Much like the message I gave to my daughter, while she thrashed about because I wasn't giving her more, as adults we also ought to spend some time focusing on the good in our life. I understand this might seem somewhat contradictory, when looking back to the SQ wish list I just asked you to write (see page 51), but it's not. It's complementary.

When you "wish" from a place of gratitude, you will always come out a winner. You are expressing positive feelings about the life you already have, while thinking about what you might like to add to this already wonderful life to enhance it even more. It is a wholly positive exploration: noting the beauty of today and hoping for even more beauty tomorrow. What a lovely way to live.

And guess what? Positive thinking, of which gratitude plays a big part, has multiple benefits, from reducing anxiety[10] to leading to greater happiness and achieving success across all areas of your life.[11] So, if you practise gratitude, you will naturally attract more good into your life.

I must say, I think the word "gratitude" has developed slightly cheesy connotations over the past few years. If you pop into a bookshop, you will often see a pastel pink gratitude journal, targeted at women, telling you about the importance of gratitude and how to journal it out. But the reason there's a market for these journals is because gratitude *matters*. Across all religions, you'll hear notes on gratitude. About not just constantly reaching and striving for more, but instead looking at what you already have and being appreciative of it.

In the Christian Bible, it says: "But blessed are your eyes because they see, and your ears because they hear" (Matthew 13:16). The Muslim Quran says: "Anyone who is grateful does so to the profit of his own soul" (31:12). The Buddhist Tipitaka says: "A person of integrity is grateful and thankful."

So there has long been an understanding that, in order to move through life peacefully, we must be thankful for all that we have already been gifted. This can be challenging when life spins us something unexpectedly difficult – like, say, a pandemic – but even in the toughest of times, we can spend a moment reflecting on all the good that remains, even with the loss we are experiencing.

---

[10] "The power of positive thinking: Pathological worry is reduced by thought replacement in Generalized Anxiety Disorder", Claire Eagleson, Sarra Hayes, Andrew Mathews, Gemma Perman and Colette R Hirsch, *Behaviour Research and Therapy*, vol. 78, March 2016

[11] "The Benefits of Frequent Positive Affect: Does Happiness Lead to Success?", Sonja Lyubomirsky and Laura King, *Psychological Bulletin*, vol. 131, no.6, 2005

For many of us, the pandemic was an incredibly testing time. Like most people, I was scared and I felt as if I couldn't protect my children in the way I wanted. However, I couldn't change the fact that it was going on, I could only learn how to cope with it. So one thing I did was develop a gratitude practice of writing a list every night before bed, about everything that I felt grateful for that day. Often, I repeated myself, but I really felt into those things I was listing.

I didn't just reel off the obvious: husband, kids and so on. If I did put my husband on the list, I would close my eyes and think about him and all that he does for me and our family, really visualize him and the good feeling I get from being with him. I'd imagine the way he holds me when we cuddle. I would picture him at the hob, cooking our family dinner. Likewise, my children: I'd think about the way they curl into my lap, the funny things that they say and how it feels when they kiss my cheek. Also, when I felt grateful for the money I was earning from my business, I thought about how I felt each time I saw that a sale had come in.

I found this gratitude listing helped me to stay focused on all that was right in my life, rather than feeling anxious about all that was wrong (and largely beyond my control). It didn't remove the anxiety – that lingered in the background – but it meant that my day-to-day felt more buoyant and fun.

As I said: I'm all about striving for more – hence the SQ wish list – but being clear on what you already have, and the value in it, matters too. Not just from a positive psychology perspective (positive psychology is the scientific study of what makes life most worth living, so it's looking for the good as we move through life), but also because being clear on what you already have – and have achieved – proves that you are capable. At one point, you probably wanted much of what you have now. So having a gratitude practice can be a form of reflection.

The first part of the gratitude exercise that follows is about returning to your beginnings and making your way forward to where you are now. And showing yourself all that you've achieved.

a) Success timeline

I'd like you to write a list of everything you have succeeded at, from birth up to now. Take your time. And remember that this doesn't all have to be around education and accolades, it can be about risks you've taken, relationships you've developed and learned from, journeys you've been on.

You might reflect on how you overcame challenges. How hard you worked on something. And the ways you've succeeded.

There are some things you probably won't feel grateful for – trauma and grief, for example – but that's not the focus here. For now, we are looking at all the stuff you can appreciate as having been a worthwhile part of your journey so far. All the things that have led you to where you're at now, the things you've done for which you feel grateful to *yourself*.

Once you've made this list, I'd like you to close your eyes and say, out loud: "I'm grateful to past me, for getting me here, to where I am now."

Now, we turn to focusing on the present.

b) Gratitude list

What, today, is good in your life?

You might think about:

- People
- Place
- Work
- Surroundings

The big stuff.

Now the minute details: fresh air coming through an open window on a hot day, sitting by a roaring log fire after a long walk in the countryside on a cold, crisp winter afternoon.

The more I think about what I'm grateful for, the more I notice the good stuff. And I note it down. It can even be things such as folded crisps (chips, in the US). Those properly crunchy crisps that have folded over in the preparation process and crack, so satisfyingly, as you bite into them. Or crunchy leaves in autumn that, when you step on them, you both feel and hear that amazing crunch. Or pulling on new cotton socks. Or a freshly-made bed.

And then, as I notice these things, I think about what I can do now, for future me, so that I can experience more of those things I already feel grateful for and that add a burst of joy to my everyday life. Like changing the sheets, or hanging out the laundry. When I get into that freshly made bed, or walk past the empty laundry basket, I feel grateful *to myself* for the gift I gave myself, by doing that thing.

I then become grateful for things happening around me every day, as well as for things I've set up for myself, as a treat or favour.

Oprah Winfrey says: "I consider gratitude to be a major force field in establishing a better life. It's the foundation from which all other blessings flow, and I want that for you, too. Something that is constantly unfolding goodness and mercy through your life is gratitude." And if you feel as if your list is a bit flat, or you've been repeating yourself and can no longer feel into each person, object or experience you're grateful for, she says: "If it feels redundant . . . you have to be specific. Not 'I'm just grateful for my health,' but 'I'm grateful that the sore throat that I had wasn't Covid.' I'm grateful that I had knee surgery and can now hike higher and faster and longer than ever before. I'm grateful not just for every breath, but I'm grateful for sinus rhythm. Here's what I've learned – it's through the worst of times that this practice of gratitude is most impactful. Of course you're grateful when things are going the way you want them to. It's during the worst of times that you need the insight to recognize your own simple abundance and to have the faith in knowing that energy is constantly changing. Your own vibrational current changes when you focus on what you have instead of what you don't."[12]

Still not sure whether it's worth creating a practice around gratitude? American professor, lecturer, author and podcast host Brené Brown says: "In [our] research, we learned that the most effective way to cultivate joy in our lives is to practice gratitude. The key word here is practice. It's not just about feeling grateful, it's about developing an observable practice. So often we think that joy makes us grateful, when in reality it's gratitude that brings joy. The data supporting this finding was so persuasive that we started a daily gratitude practice in our home. We now go around the table every night before dinner and share one thing for which we are grateful."[13].

So now have a think about what big and small things you have to be grateful for. Perhaps you could also create a practice with the people you live with and share the things you each feel grateful for at the end of day, as Brené Brown does with her family. And going forward, if you keep gratitude in mind, see if you notice more good things happening to you and those around you. Of course, it's not that more good stuff is happening, it's that your eyes are more open to it.

Here are some questions for you to ponder or journal with:

- How do you feel, having listed all that you've achieved on the success timeline?

---

[12] "Oprah on Why You Should Never Give Up on Gratitude", Oprah Winfrey, oprahdaily.com, 9 October 2022

[13] "Brené Brown on How Gratitude Begets Joy", Kon Mari, konmari.com

- How does it feel to focus on the good stuff?
- How could you incorporate more positive thinking and gratitude into your everyday?
- Is there someone you could share your thoughts with, who might like to join you in this positive reflection and gratitude?
- What one thing can you do, right now, that your future self will thank you for?

MY SQ JOURNEY

*Dr Louise Lagendijk is an Amsterdam-based integrative
medicine doctor. She's the founder of The Core – holistic
health and healing for women – and sits on the medical
board for Spinoza, who lead transformational psychedelic
experiences. Here, she talks about quitting her molecular
genetics PhD at Harvard to work one-to-one with women
in a holistic and spiritual way.*

*I graduated from medical school and went to pursue my
PhD. I wanted to do research in molecular genetics and
bioengineering, to understand the more basic cell-level
mechanisms of the uterus, which could predetermine
why women have pre-term births. I wanted to know: is it
mechanical, is it genetic, is it chemical? I wanted to get to the
bottom of it. So, during my PhD research at the Academic
Medical Centre in Amsterdam, I took out pieces of uterus
from women who were about to give birth via caesarean
section. I took them to the lab and I'd cut them and create
cells and take care of them as if they were my babies. But
I realized we'd have to find a different way of testing them,
so I went to Harvard to develop a different testing model.*

*At Harvard, I started working with Big Pharma and
I was basically looking for medications. But I realized
that, while doing this work, not only did I feel shit
myself – because the work environment at Harvard is
very unhealthy – but the people around me were also not
that healthy. I thought:* Interesting, why are doctors not
healthy?

*I've always been into preventative measures, seeing if
we can keep people healthy rather than just giving them a*

pill when they fall ill. Medication is good if you're trying to cure a patient with an acute condition, but what about all the chronic illnesses? Well, we have a problem with those, we're not really doing well in that department in western medical science.

But whenever I brought up mindfulness, for instance, my colleagues would have no time for it. It was so frustrating. We were trying to cure things with a reductionist model: looking at one organ, seeing how to target it with one specific medicine, but completely ignoring lifestyle, stress and all the many other things that go on in a person's life. Their relationships, how they think: everything that makes a human a human.

It was while I was deep in my PhD at Harvard, thinking that it didn't feel right, that I went to a talk by Tony Robbins. I followed a piece of advice he gave us in that talk: he advised making a list with two columns. On the left was about what my life was going to look like, and on the right, I had to write what I really wanted.

All the information on the right of my list was about holistic health, becoming a healer, yoga teacher, starting women's circles, being on the integrative side of medicine. I honestly thought: where did this come from? My ego was saying: stay in your lane. My heart said: go. You may not have a plan, may not know how to approach this but just go.

I remember telling my professor that I was going to leave and they told me that I was mad, and I was at the top of my career. I said: "I'm following my heart." They said: "You should follow your head." I said: "That's why I'm leaving, I can't do that." I needed to follow my heart. It was intuition. I was having an "aha" moment and I needed to follow through. It was not always easy. Leaving something behind that was so prestigious was hard for the ego.

But I left Harvard and set up The Core, which is all about women and asking: what is "the core", the root of it. The world feels different now. Now, it's person over protocol. And that's huge. I have the time to listen to people. Regular doctors have seven minutes. They are trained to work out if you're going to die or not; if you have a condition that needs to be treated immediately, or if you're at risk of cancer or some other chronic disease. But, in my field, it's all about optimizing health. We need to figure out all the little things that are unaligned. What things aren't you doing that you should be? What's your health status mentally, physically, emotionally, spiritually? It's beautiful, because I see now there are young female doctors who are coming after me who want to be educated by me.

Bringing SQ into mind–body work

I work via a system that starts with the body. If you start with meditation but have anaemia, for instance, you can't meditate yourself out of an anaemic state. If your B12 is down, you're going to feel depressed and your serotonin is going to be low, so you need to know what's going on in the body first. How is a patient's vitamin and mineral intake? Do they have food intolerances? Is their gut healthy? How are their hormones? Neurotransmitters? First, you get to the core of the body's functioning. Then you clean the body, you detox.

After that, the mind comes in. You see what the patterns are, what a patient is thinking. After that, spirit comes in.

For me, spirit has a lot to do with whether someone is aligned with what they've come here to do. Often, clients get to the end, to a point where they feel the body has been set up, we've worked on things in their mind and then they realize: hold on, maybe I want to change my job. When you clean out everything – traumas, conditioning – their intuition kicks in. People feel free to choose again.

It comes down to: "Who am I, really?" That's one of the biggest spiritual questions you can ask. And then: "What am I here to do, to give? Why have I been given this body, these lessons, what am I here to contribute, how can I serve?" That's the spiritual element, because I believe having "focus" is a highly underestimated element of health.

For me, spirit is everywhere. It's in everything. It's in the wind, in a leaf. We have the capacity to make everyday life sacred and people have different ways of doing that. When we see the small things and the interconnectedness and the beautiful intersection between the seen and the unseen, how the unseen affects the seen – how the wind affects that leaf – that is something that, if you can just be aware of it, will give life more depth. To instil that back into people, for them to become more mindful, that's very healthy. Not just for their mental wellbeing, but also for their nervous system.

Psychedelic experiences

I'm on the board of Spinoza, a psychedelics company and they work with psilocybin truffles – plant medicine – to do curated journeys for people, for the benefit of their wellbeing. I was one of the first to participate. I'm an advocate of psychedelics, I believe they can be a beautiful way to connect to self and higher self, but using them has to be done in a healthy, safe way. That's where my medical side comes in: are these potential clients on medications? On antidepressants? Is it safe for them? What's the science doing? Are there verifiable studies behind the use of psychedelics? All those things are really important to me, so I'm an ambassador for this company. The ceremonies are powerfully healing. It's subconscious work, Shamanic.

I put some of my clients on micro-dosing of psychedelics. I think it's important that we, as doctors or holistic doctors, have an understanding of the capacity of that type of medicine.

Ultimately, spirituality is a different path for everyone. I believe the future of spirituality is going to be people coming to understand that God lives within them. The guru is inside them. Psychedelics have that potency, to make you realize that, maybe, I am really you and the plant and everything around us. The psilocybin truffles come from this network in the Earth, where they are interconnected. The trees' roots talk to each other and the truffles are from those roots. So, when you take the psychedelics, you feel it. There's such deep interconnectedness between everything. That is something you don't have to be super-spiritual to understand.

Day 6. Vision-boarding

I told you earlier about "Annie's Aims", the short list I wrote, in my mid-twenties, of things I wanted to achieve (see page 29). Well, as I moved through the following years and into my thirties, I started to create a more physical, aesthetically pleasing vision of what I'd like my life to look like. Often, this included cutting images and words out of magazines, as well as writing my own words and phrases, drawing people and diagrams, or whatever else came to me creatively and intuitively.

But before I talk you through creating your own vision board, I'd like to tell you something. You may have heard about, or seen, images of Palaeolithic art work, created on the interior walls of the caves where people once lived more than 35,000 years ago, long before records began. This art has been studied by many, in a bid to determine the meaning or inspiration behind it.

French archeologists Abbé Breuil and Henri Begouën believed that prehistoric humans "attempted to influence the result of their hunt by drawing it in caves"[14]. If this is true – after all, it can only be speculation – those people were manifesting, through creating a visual representation of what they wanted to achieve. That feels quite wild and wonderful, doesn't it? The thought of these prehistoric people using rocks to create indentations in the walls of caves, to illustrate the result they'd like from their hunt. A simple life.

Now, as I walk you through creating your own vision board, remember that these people wouldn't have referred to themselves as artists or designers or illustrators. They were simply making their art because it felt lucky to do so and they were inspired. So, whether or not you think you're an artist (though I'd say we are

---

[14] "Why Did Prehistoric People Draw in the Caves?" artsandculture. google.com

all artists), it can help to sometimes stop writing or typing out lists and, instead, to draw or collage.

And I invite you to channel your inner cave dweller, as you do this exercise. Imagine the energy needed to go out and hunt for your food. The determination those people must have embodied, while also creating their art around that fact. Take that energy with you as you create your vision board, too. You could imagine that you are a cave person while you create your board, or that they are there with you, supporting and guiding you – believing in you – while you create your own version of what an ideal future looks like for you. Your ancestors, passing on hope, strength and belief as you consider what matters to you now, and going forward.

A vision board is simply a visual representation of what you'd like your life to look like. It is a sheet of card that you can lay out in front of you and see what your ideal future looks like. I've been creating my own boards for years and I like to keep them, so I can look back through them and see both what has come to fruition, and what it was that I wanted at a particular time.

For instance, in July 2018, I created a board that featured me, my husband and three children, as I was hoping to have one more baby (we had two at the time). I wrote little notes about everything I'd like to achieve (including "happiness" and "getting enough sleep"). There were images I'd cut out of magazines with women laughing, which denoted time with friends and connection, as well as words such as "calm" and "breathe" and phrases like "keep on running", because I love running. There was also an image of a wheat field, showered in golden sunlight. Now, four years later, I have three children – my youngest is three years old, he came into being a year and one month after I'd created that vision board – and I run, daily, through the fields behind my house. I feel calmer than I did when I was living in London and I do regular breathwork (see page 24). By getting clear on what

I wanted my life to look and feel like, including the shape of my family, I was able to then take the necessary steps to make that happen.

I should note that putting "having a baby" on your vision board might feel insensitive to people who are struggling to conceive, as this act of nature is so often largely out of our control. But I'm sharing it as an example of something that felt important to me, really imagining how it would feel to have a third baby . . . and then, of course, I did what you have to do to make a baby and I was lucky that, eventually, it did happen.

For your vision board, look for images that represent how you'd like to feel in your body. You might like to consider:

- Home
- Garden
- Nature
- Holidays
- People
- Food
- Smells
- Work
- Success
- Achievements
- Family
- Transport
- Clothes
- Colour
- Exercise

If you don't have paper or magazines and glue, you can also create a vision board online – there are websites specifically for creating vision boards – adding your own images. Once you've completed your vision board, download it and keep it on the desktop of your computer, or wherever you store online files. You might like to revisit it in the future and see how much of it has come to pass.

The idea behind drawing or collaging your future is that:

1. You're focusing on what it is that brings you joy, makes you feel good and would make your life feel fuller, or happier.
2. You're setting your intentions down physically, rather than just having them floating in your head, so you can refer back to them.
3. You're exploring options.

This stuff isn't set in stone once you lay it out on paper, but you're giving yourself the time to think it through creatively, rather than saying over and over again in your head: "What do I want to do with my life?" When you know you're ready to make a change, but you're not sure what that change should be, it's important to feel inspired.

The exercises below are designed to get you thinking, feeling excited, motivated and – most importantly – focusing just on yourself, for a change. There are no rules here.

Tip 1

If you get stuck and can't think of what it is that makes you feel energized, it can help to go back to childhood and think about what you loved doing as a child at, say, eight years old. Was it something active, creative, solitary, involving a team? Make a note of that activity. Think about why you loved it and how it made you feel.

As adults, we're under so much pressure to fit in: pressure from parents, partner, friends, society . . . but probably most of all from ourselves. Reflecting on what it was that gave you fire in your belly as a child can help you to ignore these expectations and reconnect with an activity that perhaps still excites you. Or to at least remember how it felt to allow yourself the space and freedom to engage with an activity you loved. Are you still doing that now? Do you have passions, hobbies and interests that excite you? If you're a tired mum or a bored employee, it can be easy to let those things slip. But here you're giving yourself permission to think freely, with no limitations.

Tip 2

While, on the whole, comparison isn't always recommended, as we're all on our own journey, when you're envisaging your dream future it can help to look around you at other people: your friends, or people you follow on social media. Whose work-life balance looks good? Why? What are they doing? This might give you some ideas about what's important to you.

Okay, so now you have looked at where you're at and where you'd like to be:

- How do you feel, looking at your vision board?
- If you were to pull out one of the things that you're working towards that you want the most, what would it be?
- What's one step you could take today towards making that a reality?
- How will it feel once you get there?
- If you look at your vision board as a whole, do the things you've put on it feel connected?
- When would you like to be living this life in its entirety?
- How will you feel when all of this has come true? You could close your eyes and imagine, for a moment – or longer – how it will feel to be living this life.
- What will your day-to-day life be like when all your dreams have come to fruition?

Quantum jumping

To move your vision-boarding into a different dimension, quite literally, you might also like to try quantum jumping. This is a practice created, or at least coined, by the late Burt Goldman, an American monk, spiritual coach and mind scientist.

Goldman became interested in spirituality and healing while on a trip to South Korea. He had a headache and so wanted to duck out of a visit to a farmhouse with his friend, but his friend insisted that he came along. He did, and when he arrived, an old man came over, put his hand to Goldman's head and the headache vanished. He couldn't believe it. When he told his friend what had happened, he laughed and explained that the old man was a Mudang, or Shaman. This enlightening experience, among others, led Goldman to explore yoga, meditation, hypnosis and hypnotherapy and he remained on this spiritual path, eventually teaching others.

But it wasn't until Goldman was in his late seventies that he started looking into physics, metaphysics and quantum physics. He learned about infinite universes and, then, about the quantum theory that this infinite sea of "bubbles" that we call universes spans both the past and the future; it transcends time. And he started to wonder why we can't travel through time, from the bubble in which we exist, to another in the past or future. "I thought, the law of physics do not apply in the world of metaphysics. In the world of metaphysics I can imagine myself on the planet Mars in an instant. The speed of light doesn't apply on the mental level. That being the case I can break through our grain of a bubble universe in an instant, and go wherever I like, whenever I like."[15].

And so it was that he found himself going into a deep meditation and imagining that he was slipping into the body of

---

[15] *Quantum Jumping*, Burt Goldman, self-published in 2013

Frank Sinatra. As he imagined Sinatra singing, he started singing himself and says that he "blew everyone away" with his vocal ability.

Now, whether or not you are ready to dive into the world of quantum physics, you might like to use the simpler version of this theory to deepen your visualization. That is, as you look at your vision board and this dream life you have laid out in front of you, you can now allow yourself to imagine that you are slipping into that future life. Close your eyes and imagine, as vividly as you can, that you are living this life.

Here are some quantum jumping prompts:

- What can you see in this visualization?
- What can you smell?
- What are you wearing and how do the clothes feel on your body?
- Who is around you?
- What sounds can you hear?

By engaging all your senses in this quantum Universe, or deep visualization, you are really feeling your way into this future life. The clearer you can become on how it feels to actually be living that life, the sooner you will be able to manifest it.

SQ EXPERIENCE: SKYCHOLOGY

It's no secret that time in nature – and away from screens – is good for us. We hear it all the time. And there are myriad studies proving the health benefits, including a Harvard paper that says 20 minutes a day in nature can actually reduce cortisol levels (that's the stress hormone).

But while we may nod in agreement and pledge to spend more time in nature, sometimes it's hard to know *how* to spend time in the great outdoors, especially if you're living in a built-up urban area. And that's where Skychology comes in.

A new area of wellbeing research, Skychology – the psychology of looking up at the sky – was developed by positive psychology coach Paul Conway. He wanted to know what we experience when we look up at the sky and how it affects our wellbeing. "I had an unhappy childhood," he says, "But found solace, peace and a greater sense of wellbeing when looking up at the sky. It helped me to feel better. I was curious to learn if there are others who feel the same." So he embarked on a research project that would determine whether this was indeed a practice that could help others, in terms of wellbeing. "It is estimated that more than 75 per cent of the world's population now live in urban environments," says Conway. "Unlike other natural environments (parks, rivers, coastline and so on), the sky is always available, wherever we are."

As hoped, Conway's study revealed that looking up at the sky is immediately calming and contributes to the experience of wellbeing.[16] It appears to be a highly effective form of emotional self-regulation, he found. It also enhances mindfulness and promotes a greater sense of connectedness and the feeling that we're part of something bigger than ourselves.

This sky-gazing practice can also lead to us experiencing awe, which Conway says is a complex emotion, linked positively to wellbeing, perspective-taking, humility, creativity, pro-social behaviour, reduced inflammatory response and enhanced immune system health. I'd add that "awe" can have spiritual connotations, too.

What's truly wonderful, though, is that the practice of staring up at the sky remains consistently effective over time, negating the effects of "hedonic adaptation", which is when positive practices stop working if we do them too often.

So, how do we get involved in Skychology?

"It can be beneficial at any time, and in any weather," says Conway. "The sky can often mirror how we are feeling, and/or remind us that everything is constantly changing, including our emotions and how we are feeling. That 'this too shall pass'. I call it 'emotional weather'."

"Transitional" skies – those at dawn and dusk – appear to be popular, he says, as are night skies. "And nothing in my research to date suggests there are times when we shouldn't look up, or any other negative effects." He has a theory that humans are physiologically wired to benefit from looking up.

---

[16] "The extraordinary in the ordinary: Skychology – an interpretative phenomenological analysis of looking up at the sky", Paul Conway, researchgate.net, March 2019

Try this:

- Stand up.
- Look directly down at your feet for ten seconds. Try to feel happy.
- Now look directly up at the ceiling/sky for ten seconds. Try to feel sad.
- What did you notice?

Quick tips for sky-gazing from Skychologist Paul Conway

Commit one minute each day to pause and look up at the sky. Think of it as "me-time" when you can hit the reset button and feel a greater sense of calm and inner peace:

- Stand, sit, or lie down in a comfortable position where you can see as much sky as possible.
- Take a few nice deep breaths: in through the nose, out through the mouth.
- Notice what you see. Shapes, movement, stillness, colour, contrast . . .
- Allow thoughts and feelings to come and go.
- Look at the sky as long as you like. I recommend at least 60 seconds if you can.
- When ready, finish with one more nice deep breath: in through the nose, out through the mouth.
- Notice how you feel.
- What feels different from before you stopped to look up at the sky?

Day 7. Manifesto

As we come to the end of this seven-day self-coaching practice on designing your dream life, I'd like to invite you to do one last exercise: create your own manifesto about how you'd like to live your life. This is something that we might do as business owners, in terms of what we promise to do as a company, but less often as individuals. However, committing to a series of statements, or declarations, about who we are and who we'd like to be, can help us to move into the highest version of ourselves.

Before writing your manifesto, you might like to close your eyes, place a hand on your heart and take some nice deep breaths: inhale through your nose; sigh loudly and unashamedly as you exhale through your mouth. Ask yourself: "Who am I, and who do I want to be?"

So, are you ready to create your own manifesto? Here's mine.

Annie's Manifesto for Life:

- I write daily.
- I am bold.
- I am creative.
- I have big dreams.
- I believe in magic.
- I am whole and capable.
- I trust and collaborate with fellow women.
- I value work, rest and play.
- I say "yes" even if it feels scary.
- I say "no" if it's not right for me.
- I celebrate the successes of others.
- I am healthy in body, mind and spirit.
- I take regular breaks.

MY SQ JOURNEY
Gaby Power is a freelance producer for bands including Gorillaz, and a manifestation coach.

We were brought up as Catholic, though didn't regularly go to church. My mum always had crystals around the house but never really spoke about it: they were just like ornaments. It's only in the last couple of years that I've realized she would have classed herself as quite a hippie and she does believe in all that stuff. So it's always been in the background.

My dad introduced me to Buddhism when I was 16. I've been practising for around ten years now. I never really aligned with Catholicism or going to church, I found churches really haunting. But Buddhism is a philosophy of life. There's no right and wrong. That feels more aligned than any "rule book". It's that oneness of self and environment, so what you put out is what you're going to get back. And that happens whether we like it or not. That ties in with manifestation beliefs and the law of attraction: what you put out, you get back. It's like gravity, it's just a law. It feels right.

I've always been dedicated to my routines because, if I let them slip, I feel like everything goes off track. With Buddhism, I dip in and out of the actual practice, but the sentiment lives within my heart. But, generally, I would chant "Namu Myōhō Renge Kyō" – Japanese words chanted within all forms of Nichiren Buddhism – and do a prayer called gongyo, which is praying for the peace and happiness of the world and everyone around you and yourself. It sums up what you want to develop in your human evolution. It keeps you growing and bettering yourself and changes your karma for the better. It's a lovely practice. There's so much science behind the benefits of chanting itself: the vibration of saying a chant lights up the electrolytes in your body, it shifts something and it's so powerful.

Daily SQ routine

I have to wake up and journal every morning. I free-write, but essentially I log how I'm feeling. Whether I'm stressed about something or I'm really happy, I try and take a minute to tune in and observe what's going on within me. If I don't journal, I feel like I've ignored myself and been sucked in by the world. So it's really important to me.

The music industry is really stressful and sometimes we get caught up in it. I'm very visual, so in the morning, I imagine I'm putting on a "positivity cloak". I see it like Harry Potter's invisibility cloak. No one can take it off me. We're all going to come across stressful people – on the roads, on the way to work, at the gym, on the train – but the cloak means people can't penetrate our vibe. If you let them in, that will send you on a downward spiral. But if you have this bubble of love, compassion and being grounded and balanced, they can't get in; you just reflect it back. So, when people project on to you and you're wearing your positivity cloak, you don't take it in and let it get into your skin. Instead, it rolls off you.

A new part of my routine is "tapping" – physically tapping on meridian points around my body – an emotional freedom technique (EFT). I absolutely love it. I've always struggled to meditate, but tapping works for me. I can do it at any time in the day, but I try to do it in the morning, as it's really great for lowering your cortisol levels. I have endometriosis and PCOS (polycystic ovarian syndrome), so my cortisol levels are always quite high and hard to balance, but I can feel the sense, across my whole body, that there's a change after I tap.

Also, if I've had a stressful meeting, I'll come out and tap for two minutes, then I'm balanced. It dissipates stress, it's a really powerful practice that you can do anywhere.

How a high SQ has helped me to succeed

I attribute all my success to spirituality. I left school at 16 and landed an apprenticeship at national broadcaster Channel 4 out of the blue. I ended up working there for four or five years, in a role inspiring young people to take alternative routes into careers and training them up. I loved that. And that's when I got into Buddhism.

While at Channel 4, I realized that I wanted to get into music. I got invited on to a local radio station to talk about my job working with young people in the media industry. And I thought: Ooh, I love this, I want to stay. I really believe in the law of attraction, but a big part of that is the "action" element: you have to do your part of the bargain and the rest will follow. So I reached out to the radio station and asked if there was anything I could do there. If I ever want to do something, I just ask, I never feel nervous and that's been key for me. Soon, I was producing a radio show and that's where I met my partner Munya. I've been with him for six years now.

I wrote a list of six people I could contact who might be able to help me work in music. I met up with two of them, then I got a call from the radio station to let me know there was an artist management role available for Gorillaz. I thought: This looks good. *I applied for it and got it. Everything I set out to do happens quite quickly; it's the power of intention. I worked with Gorillaz for a few years, then I left to do a coaching course, launched my coaching business, worked with 50 people in the first year and then decided I needed a balance of creative with the coaching, I missed the media side of things.*

Now, I really tap into those manifestation techniques every week, because with freelancing, if I'm in a negative mindset, I notice that everything goes a bit quiet; the work dries up. I start to let those limiting beliefs in, such as: Maybe I'm just not that good, *or,* Maybe there isn't anything going on. *But as soon as I say: "This week I want to manifest two freelance jobs, thank you, Universe," literally hours later I get work. Something happens, without fail, every time.*

At the moment, I'm juggling about five different freelance clients, which is really exciting and a bit overwhelming, but I'm just really grateful that every time I ask, I receive. I would absolutely attribute these opportunities to the law of attraction. Tuning into it and seeing yourself as a magnet, when you ask. It's all already there; there are already opportunities, it's just about drawing them in. My friends all call me a manifesting witch.

My SQ toolkit

Journal. *I carry it with me wherever I go, in case I need to hit the page.*

Crystals. *In every handbag, I have one – an amethyst, clear quartz, rose quartz. They're like protection for me. I always have one in my car, too. I wash them, put them under a new moon to charge, keep them next to my bed. I take comfort in knowing they're there, like a portable charger. If I'm low, they're there beside me to give me an extra boost.*

Something for each of the five senses:

- *Smell: I always have a lavender or lemongrass balm or spray to smell.*
- *Touch: A soft, fleecy blanket that I bought in lockdown and it feels like my "safe" material; if I feel overwhelmed or stressed it's like a hug from the Universe.*
- *Taste: I love a mint tea, or normal tea, for taste. As my mum says, a cup of tea always helps.*
- *See: Being out in nature, going for a walk, having a view of trees from my office.*

- *Hear: I like to listen to subliminals, which is audio with affirmations built in and there are binaural beats that you can't always hear. It's really calming.*

SQ books I'd recommend

The Magic *by Rhonda Byrne*
This book is a 30-day gratitude practice. You read a chapter a day and it focuses on different things you have to be grateful for. It might be about being grateful for all the things you had as a child: school uniform, lunch money. That helps you to work through money blocks from the past that are blocking you now from financial abundance. I do this practice every January and once in the middle of the year.

Positively Wealthy: A 33-day guide to manifesting sustainable wealth and abundance in all areas of your life *by Emma Mumford*
This book contains different manifestation techniques. I wake up excited to read it and focus on something positive that morning.

The Miracle Morning: The 6 habits that will transform your life by 8am *by Hal Elrod*
This book has six tasks for you to do when you first wake up: silence, affirmations, visualization, exercise, reading and scribing. Ten minutes of each. It works so well for me.

USING AYURVEDA TO BETTER UNDERSTAND YOUR PERSONALITY

Do you ever feel as though everyone around you has more energy? Or perhaps you wonder why you find it hard to relax? Well, the ancient life science of Ayurveda – which translates as "knowledge of life" – might be just the tool you need. Here, Ayurvedic practitioner Sureta Puri explains how it works . . .

This ancient Indian life science helps us to understand how our constitution – known in Ayurveda as dosha – affects all aspects of our life, health and wellbeing.

Ayurvedic principles are governed by the five elements: earth, water, air, fire and ether. We are all composed of a combination of these and the balance will signify our dosha. When we understand our dosha, we can balance our lives to maximize our wellness.

There are three doshas: vata, which is comprised of air and ether; pitta, which is made up of fire and water; and kapha, which is formed of water and earth. Everyone has a different ratio of each dosha, usually with one more prominent, that influences physiological, emotional and mental health. Each manifests in different ways.

Do you have a meltdown if you can't fit in your intense workout routine? You might be vata.

Are you driven by being the best, while doing everything perfectly? This is a pitta trait.

Or, perhaps you have less drive and motivation and prefer a slower pace of life? Hello, kapha.

Vata people tend to be active, creative and spacey. However, they can also get anxious and be over-thinkers.

Their natural body shape is slim and they typically prefer raw, cold, dry foods.

Pitta individuals are fiery and passionate, goal-driven people. This heat can also create jealousy and anger. Their natural build is athletic and they gravitate towards spicy and oily foods.

Kapha types are supporting and caring, but can suffer from a lack of motivation, depression and sluggishness. They are often bigger-boned and enjoy warming, comforting foods.

Illnesses are signs of an imbalanced dosha. For example, eczema is a drying vata imbalance, inflammation is a heating pitta imbalance and congestion is a damp kapha imbalance.

Ayurveda addresses imbalances through diet, herbal remedies and lifestyles. This is why it is important to understand how each dosha presents itself. You can do a dosha test online, but to fully understand your natural constitution and any imbalances, it is recommended that you consult with a qualified Ayurvedic practitioner or doctor.

In the west, we live in a highly pitta-dominated society. Being pushed to excel, to work hard, to succeed and be perfect. Stress is normalized and our minds – and bodies – easily overheat. Even the increasing global temperatures are a sign of pitta's heat. This work-hard mentality is perfect for pitta people, but what about the spontaneous vatas or leisurely kaphas?

By understanding the natural flow of your dosha, you can live a life that is manageable for you. This knowledge and awareness can enable you to find your groove and bring balance, instead of trying to keep up with behaviours that are not conducive for you.

To dig deeper, let's explore what typically works – and does not – for each dosha:

Vata people tend to love running, cycling and HIIT workouts. However, if imbalanced, they should opt for pacifying activities such as meditation and slower-paced yoga. This might seem hellish to vata people, as they love to burn energy and be on the go, but it is important to slow down and be present. Never try to box in that spontaneity though: let vatas fly, otherwise they will feel trapped.

Pitta people are naturally competitive, so team sports are great for them. Although they should not exercise in the heat – or do hot yoga – as that will only increase their natural fire. Instead, calming and cooling activities should be the focus. Pittas will always work hard, but they must take regular breaks to avoid burnout. Listening to calm music and bringing in regular breathwork practice will help to slow the mind.

Kapha people can be quite solitary figures, which is okay: it is important for them to have alone time and not feel pressured to constantly socialize. They sometimes need motivation, so exercising with a friend is beneficial. Kaphas should go at a pace that works for them and not feel pressured to be part of the fast modern lifestyle. Embracing change can take time with them, but everything they do will be done with commitment.

So listen to your body. Tune into what does and does not feel good. Reflect on changes you experience through certain activities, foods and seasons and find what works for you. And get ready to feel empowered.

Which dosha sounds most like you?

3

YOUR DAILY SQ ROUTINE

Before giving birth to my first baby eight years ago, I was a full-time copywriter for a film company in London. I liked writing copy for adverts, but the 9am–6pm routine had started to take its toll. I remember, one morning, waking abruptly to my alarm and thinking: *This is like Groundhog Day.* My alarm went off at 6am, I got up and went for a run, had a quick shower, grabbed some breakfast and then tackled the busy, stressful commute to work. And, once I'd arrived at the office, the days took on a similar pattern of (often unnecessary) meetings, a rushed sandwich for lunch, then a slow afternoon of noticing my colleagues clock-watching. That morning, I thought: *Will I be doing this forever?*

But then I became pregnant and not only was it the end of that job, but it was, for me, the end of office work.

While there had been comfort in knowing what I was doing each day – and getting a regular pay cheque in return – I didn't like the actual routine. It was dull, monotonous and there was rarely any joy. I would jostle for space on the underground to start and end my day and I didn't yet even realize that I could inject spiritual energy into my working life. But, when I started working for myself, things began to change. For the first time in my working life, I was in charge of how my day looked. I didn't have to rush to my desk for 9am if I had been working late the night before, or if I had a bad night with the kids. Of course, I needed to put the hours in, but I didn't have to clock in at the behest of someone else. I got really excited about finding ways to make even the most mundane admin day more fun, and that's all down to incorporating SQ into my working day.

Now, I've designed a morning routine that makes me feel excited and invigorated for the day ahead, because how you start your day impacts the rest of it. A study has shown that people with a positive outlook will be more productive, hopeful and dedicated to their work.[17] So it makes sense that getting up and focusing on the good in your life, and what exciting things might happen that day, will have a positive impact on how the day pans out.

But it's not just the morning I've curated for optimum peace and joy, it's the whole day. Rather than moving sluggishly or resentfully through my days, I have taken charge. I am clear on what gives me energy, what helps me to relax, what I need if I'm feeling self-doubt slipping in and what tools work best for guiding me if I have a big decision to make. These are all spiritual tools, of course.

Whether you work in an office or from home, if you're your own boss or work for someone else, creating a daily SQ routine will transform your working life. Instead of feeling like you just need to get through to Friday so that you can relax, you'll start to enjoy every day more. Since creating my own SQ routine three years ago, I might be sitting down to do a tax return or pay invoices, but I will feel enthused and light, because of the rituals and routine I have created that precede and follow this task.

---

[17] "Good morning, good day: A diary study on positive emotions, hope, and work engagement", Else Ouweneel, P M Le Blanc, Wilmar B Schaufeli and Corine I van Wijhe, *Human Relations*, vol. 65, issue 9, September 2012

Your SQ starter kit

The secret of an SQ routine lies in the small, simple practices you can incorporate into your everyday life to boost your energy levels and self-belief. If you stick to these, I guarantee you'll feel your spirits lift over time. There are certain objects that are integral to my daily SQ routine however; so, to start, I'm going to make some suggestions for your SQ starter kit.

You will need:

Incense. I use mine like a wand, to cleanse a space such as my office or living room before I start work every day, and often a few times throughout the day too. I love nag champa (a calming, soothing fragrance of Indian origin, made from a combination of sandalwood and champak) but you might like to go to a shop and find a scent that works for you.

A scented candle. This can be used for prayer and affirmation, or to keep lit while you work (especially at night-time or in the winter months). Every year, for my birthday, my husband buys me a candle with aromas of cypress, cedar and vetiver. It smells heavenly to me. Again, you might like to go into a shop so that you can have a good sniff and see what scents you feel most drawn to. Equally, you can use a simple tea light for spells and rituals, using the flame to focus your prayers and affirmations on.

Tarot cards. We'll go into more detail about both tarot and oracle cards later (see page 191), but I find the journey to finding the right pack of tarot for you to be a personal one. I picked up my favourite pack of tarot cards in a beautiful shop in London on a bright, sunny day. I loved the ethereal illustrations on the deck and it just felt right. My latest box came from my sister; I asked her to buy me a deck for my birthday, as I knew she'd find some special cards as we're very close and spiritually aligned. If you're buying for yourself, you can go to a spiritual shop or look online. See which pack you're drawn to. Some packs have longer descriptions of each card, which I like, but you might prefer the shorter ones, favouring the illustration over text to guide your reading.

A collection of gemstones. I like to buy these in person and feel them in the palm of my hand, because the way I use them is very much about the way they feel. My favourite shop is in Lyme Regis, on the UK's Dorset coast (see page 269), but you can order gemstones from a variety of shops online. Choose the colours you feel drawn to, or look into the meaning of each stone. For instance, rose quartz is believed to bring love, while green jasper stones are said to represent calm and tranquillity. If you're feeling unsure about what stones to choose for your SQ starter kit, I'd recommend rose quartz (for love), clear quartz (for manifestation and intention) and jade (for luck and wealth). (For gemstones for work success, see page 144.)

Your SQ starter kit might look different to mine and that's completely fine. After all, we are each on our own individual journey. We will be drawn towards different scents and, if you buy gemstones in person, how they feel in your palm – the size and shape that feels right for you – will depend on the size and shape of your hand. But remember that, in purchasing each of the items above, you will be using your intuition to guide you towards that which feels right. This is a spiritual intelligence-boosting exercise in itself. So enjoy the process and let your intuition guide you on the first step of your SQ journey. Once you have your SQ starter kit, you're ready to move on to the next step.

The power of mindset

Now, while I believe that anyone can improve their working day by incorporating spiritual tools into their routine, it's important to note that mindset plays a part, too. Remember the study I mentioned earlier, about how starting the day with a positive mindset improves the whole day, in terms of productivity? Well, this is a great example of positive psychology: the scientific study of what makes life most worth living[18]. It's about focusing on our strengths rather than our weaknesses and on those small moments in our day that bring us joy, as well as honing in on positive states (compassion, kindness, resilience) and experiences (feeling love or happiness). We can easily let these positive moments go by, but, when we choose to really see and experience them, our overall happiness levels increase.

So, in terms of your daily SQ routine, it all starts with how you get out of bed first thing in the morning. We absolutely have a choice about how we approach the day ahead. We can wake up and think: *Urgh, I can't be bothered to get up.* Or we can create a more positive dialogue in our head.

Here's an example of a negative approach to the day beginning. When my husband and I first moved in together, he was working at a job he hated. Every morning, after being woken by his alarm, he'd sing: "I gotta get, I gotta get up, I gotta get up. Don't wanna get up, don't wanna get up, don't wanna get up." This was a pretty grumbly and "low vibe" way to start the day. By "low vibe", I mean negative, low in energy, moany and not conducive to wonderful things happening, as opposed to "high vibe", which is all about excitement, big energy, vibrancy, positivity.

---

[18] "What Is Positive Psychology & Why Is It Important?" Courtney E Ackerman, positivepsychology.com, 20 April 2018

So there is a choice to be made: do you adopt the positive psychology school of thought and focus on the good? Or do you opt for the "learned helplessness" concept, coined by psychologist Martin Seligman in the 1960s, which is where humans learn to become helpless and feel they have lost control over what happens to them.[19] I'm guessing we all like the sound of the former, of choosing to think thoughts and take actions that make us feel happier rather than depleted.

But it can sometimes feel as if we're swimming against the tide, when there are common phrases such as "getting out on the wrong side of bed", which suggest that having a bad day is simply beyond our control. It's as if we're assigning the fate of our day to some unknown higher power and so we get up, assuming the day is going to be rubbish. We wake up feeling tired and irritated and we then go on to notice every "bad" thing that happens that day. Perhaps you sit up, hit your head, swing your legs round and put your foot on something sharp, you walk downstairs to make your morning coffee only to be greeted with curdled milk, stale bread and so on and so forth, all the way until bedtime.

But how about getting out on the right side of bed every day? Because we do have a choice. You get to decide, at the start of each day, how you'd like to approach the day ahead. You can go in on a low vibe: *Urgh, I don't want to get up*, or choose a high vibe: *Today is going to be good*. This all comes down to your mindset.

On waking, I like to begin my day by lying still and taking a moment to think about what I'm looking forward to that day, or what I'll be spending my time doing, and creating an affirmation – a short, positive statement – around this. So, I might think something like: *I'm excited for the meeting with*

---

[19] "Failure to escape traumatic shock", M E Seligman and S F Maier, *Journal of Experimental Psychology*, vol. 74, issue 2, May 1967

my publisher, it's going to lead to good things. I then get up and head downstairs for my morning coffee, hoping that if I'm quiet I won't wake anyone else up and I can enjoy half an hour of quiet time, ready to embrace the day ahead.

Tip: keep a notebook by your bed, as you might like to use it for morning journaling as well as for a gratitude practice at the beginning or end of the day.

If you like to wake slowly in the morning, you could light a scented candle or a scent diffuser with an oil that makes you feel relaxed, happy or energized, depending on how you like to start the day. As the fragrance fills the room, lie back and enjoy the waves of scent floating around you. A strong scent can create a mindful meditation, as it engages the senses and focuses your mind on the task at hand. This could be an opportunity to practice some breathwork, too.

When your mind reactivates, you can then create a morning affirmation to help set an intention for the day ahead.

Here are my top five morning affirmations I use to start my day:

- Today is going to be a good day.
- All good things come to me.
- I am calm, collected, confident and successful.
- Something magical is going to happen today.
- I can do this.

By consistently starting your day with a positive affirmation, you are setting yourself up for success. That is, you are preparing yourself for a brilliant day ahead rather than letting the negative thoughts and worries dictate how the day will pan out. Over time, you will actually rewire your brain. This is called neuroplasticity and it's the brain's ability to change, adapt and form new neural connections as a result of experience. This rewiring can affect your life going forward, leading to positive growth and change.[20] If you allow negative thoughts to take over, your brain's circuits get caught up in negative narratives, but equally, if you choose to select positive thoughts, experiences and expectations, you will find yourself feeling more positive about life.

It should be noted that, when things are particularly difficult at work, it might feel disingenuous to say: "This is going to be an incredible day, I am wonderful." But you could try affirmations such as: "I am capable, I am loved, I can do this." Adopting a positive psychological approach and weaving in SQ tools is a simple method when you need a small boost, but when experiencing any kind of trauma, it isn't always realistic to list everything that is amazing about your life, or to expect a "beautiful, magical" day. Instead, it can help to adopt a mindset of acceptance and to opt for getting through the day as best you can. So, when you're in a really difficult place, you can use these affirmations to help elevate you to feeling good enough to get through the day. Once you have worked through the challenging period, you can think about elevating yourself to a higher state of joy by really focusing on the more powerful affirmations, firm in the belief that the day truly will be magical.

This might seem like a mindset exercise more than a spiritual one, but the two are connected. Reaching for hope and belief about the day ahead requires a certain amount of faith. To take it to the next level, though, you might also like to ask a higher being to support you with this intention (for more on affirmation, prayer and spells, see page 215). Having spiritual beliefs starts in the mind; believing in something bigger than ourselves – whether you see it as a god or an "energy" surrounding you – takes a certain amount of faith and optimism. As discussed, a positive mindset

[20] "Rewiring Your Brain for Positivity with 'Mature Gratitude'", Andrea Rice, psychcentral.com, 23 November 2021

is crucial for our everyday and longer-term health, but taking it a step further and asking for guidance from a deity is where the magic truly happens. This is what elevates these practices from being simple meditations and transforms them to a spiritual level.

The start of your day is also a great point to bring in your gemstones. If the sun is out, why don't you lay your gemstones in the sunlight, on your windowsill, while you shower and get ready, as this charges them with energy. If you've selected a gemstone such as clear quartz – one of the ultimate crystals for giving you energy – then by leaving it under direct sunlight, your stone is getting charged up, meaning that, when you take it in your palm, you can start to absorb some of that energy and feel yourself, in turn, become energized.

I also like to include some movement, such as stretching, while saying my affirmations. This allows me to stay fully present in my body and mind, without getting distracted. As I say my affirmations, while lying on my back, pulling my knees into my chest and rocking gently from side to side, I say the words out loud, in time with the rocking. While doing this, I am there in the room with my thoughts, absorbing those words, truly believing the intention behind them. You could also try taking a walk out in nature, if that's possible, using the rhythm of your footsteps to repeat your mantra or affirmation over and over again. You really do need to lean into those words until you truly believe them. Say them out loud, say them quietly, say them in your head, but just don't say them thoughtlessly. Try different things and see what works for you. Perhaps it will be a combination.

SQ in the world
Artists on SQ

The renowned artists below reference SQ in their work, suggesting it is a fundamental part of their creative expression.

"Art is the path to being spiritual."

Piet Mondrian

"Where the spirit does not work with the hand, there is no art."

Leonardo da Vinci

"The painting has a life of its own. I try to let it come through."[21]

Jackson Pollock

"That is beautiful which is produced by the inner need, which springs from the soul."

Wassily Kandinsky

"I need art like I need God"[22]

Tracey Emin

"You get whatever accomplishment you are willing to declare."

Georgia O'Keeffe

"Everyone needs a fantasy."

Andy Warhol

---

[21] "My Painting", Jackson Pollock, *Possibilities I*, Winter 1947–48
[22] Exhibition at South London Gallery, 16 April–18 May 1997

Workday SQ routine

Whether you're commuting into work or heading to a home office, you now have an opportunity to set an intention for your working day. How would you like to feel as you work? You might like to feel calm, focused, productive or present, or a combination.

Once you are at your desk, list all the things that make you happy, whether or not they are in your life and happening right now. Why not treat yourself to a dedicated notebook for happiness reflections and for setting happiness goals? The aim here is to focus on what you want, and love, rather than what you don't want. Just like choosing to get out of bed and saying something positive and upbeat, by looking at the things that make you smile and feel good in your mind and body – and working towards having more of these things, people and experiences – you are choosing to move towards a life of abundance.

Think about the different areas of your life (relationships, work, home, hobbies, free time, health) and what makes you happy in each area. List these out, thinking of as many things as you can. It can be fleeting moments such as hearing birds tweeting first thing in the morning, as well as the bigger things like going for a candlelit romantic dinner with your partner. Perhaps long beach holidays abroad make you happy, holding hands with your child, or cuddling up with a friend in front of a film. And then get clear on what it is about that experience or object that makes you happy and how to inject more of it into your life.

Prompts for happiness journaling:

- Three things that make me happy are . . .
- I like them because . . .
- I want more . . . in my life.
- If I had that, I could . . .
- One step I could take towards achieving that is . . .

- I intend to do that by [time/date].
- When I have, I'll feel . . .

As I explained earlier, "the law of attraction" dictates that focusing on what you want attracts more of it into your life. Rhonda Byrnes, who popularized this term in her book *The Secret*, talks about the Universe being made up of energy, and so you attract more of what you focus on. If you fixate on how annoying someone is being, you will attract more annoying people into your life, but if you focus on how beautiful a rose smells, you will attract more beautiful flowers and experiences into your life. While some people are cynical about the law of attraction, simply put, if you are focusing on good things, you will feel better in yourself and this means people will respond to you in a more positive way. Most of us feel more drawn to a friendly person than to someone who constantly moans. That is a simple example of how focusing on the good attracts more of it into your life.

While doing my own happiness journaling at the beginning of a working day, I often plug in a scent diffuser, releasing a happy fragrance (a scented oil designed specifically to make you feel happy) and I imagine the steam rising and molecules of positivity floating all around my office. If you use your scent diffuser earlier on in your morning routine, you can instead light a stick of incense and waft it around your desk and the room you're working in. As I do this, I repeat a positive affirmation phrase such as: "This is going to be a good working day." Or if I'm doing something specific such as making a telephone call first thing, I will say: "This call is going to be amazing, it will lead to great things."

I will then "dong" my Tibetan singing bowl and I like to wait until the sound has completely disappeared before I sit down to work. This acts as a reminder to slow down. Stop rushing. Wait the minute or two until the sound has drifted away, rather than stilling the bowl and its resonant sound. This isn't wasted time, it's meditative and peaceful and the act is in itself a form of intention-setting: I'm not going to rush, I'm going to go slowly and steadily as I wait until one task is finished before starting another.

If you don't have a Tibetan singing bowl (and you don't fancy investing in one, as they are pretty niche) you could find a "dong" sound online and use that instead. Either way, this exercise is about approaching your day with a calm, focused energy rather than manically rushing into work, a half-eaten piece of toast in hand, opening up your emails feeling stressed and rushed. We want to approach the working day, and life in general, from a place of calm competence.

After this, I sit down to work in my space feeling as though I'm surrounded by good energy.

For those working in a shared office space, there may be some limitations in terms of lighting candles and creating your own sounds; a round of chanting or "dong-ing" a Tibetan singing bowl while colleagues discuss their weekend shenanigans might be taking it a step too far . . . But there are ways to find peace and focus when others are working loudly around you. It starts with a tranquil space, so set up your work desk shrine using the ideas you'll find in Chapter 4 (see page 133). See your work desk as a sacred space for creation. Whatever line of work you're in, there will be creativity involved in terms of coming up with new ideas, innovating and how you relate to those around you. And any time you feel overwhelmed, or bored, you can reach for your gemstones, close your eyes and say a line in your mind about what you'd like next. Here are some ideas:

- Bring me back into this moment.
- Give me new ideas.
- I am ready to innovate; guide me.

By adopting a mindset of acceptance, I've managed to work much of my freelance writing career in building sites. Instead of letting the hammer drill fill me with fury, I accept it as background noise and focus on the computer in front of me. But others might appreciate a pair of sound-cancelling headphones instead . . .

Energy dip

If, at any point in the day, I feel my energy or confidence dip – perhaps after a long video call or the classic mid-afternoon slump – I reach for a gemstone. I will move away from my computer and hold a gemstone, or a selection of them, in the palm of my hand, rolling them around like worry beads. I close my eyes while enjoying the feel of the smooth stones in my palm and I'll either still my mind or ask for guidance. Perhaps I'll say: "Help me to find calmness." Or I'll give acknowledgement and thanks for my day so far, asking for momentum to carry on, with phrases such as: "I am doing well today," or, "Thank you for guiding me in my work."

At times, I won't feel much, so I'll rinse my gemstones. This simple cleansing ritual is believed to clean the stones, re-energizing them: an alternative to the morning sunlight, or the full moon methods (see pages 107 and 120). If you're still feeling lost when I am talking about the stones having "energy", this is energy I assign to them. I imagine that, beyond the traditional meaning they have been given – if you buy a gemstone, it will often be accompanied by a note declaring its meaning, for instance, rose quartz is believed to bring love – these stones are emanating their own energy just for me. Choosing to believe in the power of a gemstone and its properties is raising your SQ. You are choosing to believe that, by holding that particular gemstone in your hand, at that moment, you are connecting to something bigger than yourself; to an external energy that emanates from that stone. We have power over our minds and our thoughts; we have power over our bodies and our physical actions; but this belief in an external energy is adding a spiritual connection, a faith in a power that lies beyond body and mind. And once this clicks and you allow yourself to sink into this belief, well, that's when the magic truly begins.

Some days, though, I will find certain tools work better than others. If I've rolled my gemstones around in my palm and asked for guidance, but I still don't feel I have clarity – or if I continue to feel overwhelmed – that's when I will move away from my desk and my office space and go for a walk. When I lived in London, I would walk around the streets or go to a park. I like to be surrounded by green, whether it's wild or landscaped. It calms my mind. In fact, it calms all of us; exposure to nature has been proven to reduce anxiety, to lower cortisol levels and to help with sleep. To bring in the spiritual powers of nature, you can imagine that, wherever you are, there are fairies hiding in the tress or bushes, behind the sand dunes or in the riverbed reeds. When out in nature, ask the fairies – in your head, or out loud – to help you find the answer you need. Really, the answer is always within you, but turning outwards and relying on an imagined outside entity to guide you to the answer can often help to unblock your mind.

I'll then return to work and keep going until I feel my energy is disappearing for the day.

At the end of the day, if I've had difficult conversations, or feel my work hasn't gone as I'd like, I might burn some nag champa incense to dispel the negative energies from the space, so I can return the next morning to a fresh and cleansed office. As I light the incense, I'll imagine that the air is full of negative energy that might look like smoke, general darkness or dust particles. Whatever it is, it's imagined, but by picturing these negative feelings as something tangible in the air, it feels easier to clear them. Much like sweeping actual dirt out of the kitchen, I am sweeping my mind of these negative thoughts. As I wave the incense wand around, I imagine I am bringing a fresh, positive energy into the same air. I will ask the negative energies of the day to go before calling in positive energies, saying: "All negative energies can go now, I welcome positive energies back in."

After dinner, I clear the kitchen and light a candle, which I place on the dining room table. Before putting on music to have a dance and sing with my kids, I sit down – alone, if possible – and focus on the flame of the candle and the scent. I lean in towards it to get a good sniff. And then I say something about being thankful for the day or about what I hope for the next day. If my kids are hanging around, I'll invite them to join me and, if they don't fancy coming up with something themselves, I'll say something such as: "Thank you for today, for all the good moments, and goodbye to the trickier ones, we will leave them here. Tomorrow is going to be wonderful." And I always make a wish when I blow out the candle. (That bit my kids will always join in with, so, especially in winter, I end up lighting lots more candles so that there's one for everyone to blow out.)

Glum days

We all have them. Those days where it feels as though nothing is quite right. Perhaps your usual boosts aren't working, or you can't even remember what they are. On these days, it can help to remind yourself of all that is going right (even if it all feels wrong). So here are seven journal prompts to turn to when life is feeling sticky or glum or low and you need to remind yourself that you are capable, doing well and have the power and support to make positive changes.

- One thing that is going well for me is . . .
- Something I've achieved recently is . . .
- One thing I'd like to change is . . .
- I'm grateful for . . .

- I need help with . . .
- Someone I can turn to is . . .
- How I want to feel . . .

Wind-down routine

Before discovering the power of SQ, I used to wait until I felt really tired before going to bed, often to the point of falling asleep in front of the TV. It meant that, once I'd cleaned my teeth and got into bed, I'd crash. Now, I try to be more intentional with how I end my day, as I believe our days should be bookended with positive rituals. In the same way that we want to start the day feeling excited and upbeat – which leads to a calmer, more productive day – we want to end the day feeling accomplished and relaxed, leading to better sleep, which is crucial for our mental and physical health.

Before bed every night, I write a list of everything I'm grateful for. I'll keep a notebook by my bed and list as many things as I can think of. If I'm feeling stressed, tired or low in energy, I might just write down three things, but otherwise, I'll take my mind back to the start of the day and write each and every moment I found gratitude in. When writing down each moment, I will try to really focus on it. So, if I'm feeling grateful for my morning coffee (this regularly comes up), I'll imagine the taste of that coffee and how it feels while I'm drinking it, the energy I get from the caffeine and all the ideas that come flowing in. When you see it and feel it, you believe it.

Some other things that regularly feature on my gratitude list are: running, feeling safe, money, comfortable clothes, a crisp salad or a delicious meal. Your gratitude list shouldn't be a list of all the life-changing, expensive or rare experiences, mostly it's the really small, everyday exchanges or magical moments that make my life that little bit better. Perhaps you could consider:

- Five people you feel grateful for.
- A recent opportunity that has felt exciting (such as an interview, conversation, pay rise, new venture).
- Three things that happened today that gave your spirits a boost.
- Is there a part of your routine that you love?
- What do you have coming up that you feel grateful for?

To end the day, I like to create an intention for the following day, so that I wake up feeling clear on what I'd like to achieve. And then I have a lovely sleep (as long as none of my children wake me up).

If you're finding yourself scrolling on social media right up until shut-eye, try leaving your phone in a different room. We really don't need to be checking what the rest of the world is up to right until we drop off to sleep. Ideally, an hour of no screens before bed helps you to wind down more naturally. Also, when your phone isn't lying next to your pillow, it won't be the first thing you reach for in the morning. That said, if you're looking for a tech-based sleep aid, there are calmness and mindfulness apps that offer meditations to send you off into restful slumber.

Raise your vibe

When living a high SQ life, or working on raising your SQ, you will be living what is more commonly referred to as a "high vibe" life. This is the best place from which to manifest and to generally feel better in your day-to-day life and at work. There are certain activities that will help you to move into a "high vibe", while others will lower your vibe. Here are some ideas . . .

High vibe

People who encourage you	Singing
Time in nature	Sleep
Intuitive eating	Reading uplifting books
Dancing	Outfits that feel good
Comedy	Learning
Celebrating	Music
Gifts to yourself	New Experiences

The news	Tiredness
People who make fun of you	Too much screen time
Dieting	People who put you down
Doom scrolling	Binge drinking
Hunger	Panicking
Lack of sleep	Putting yourself last

Low vibe

Cleansing your home

Over the years, I've lived in many a haunted house. And while I'm getting used to accepting these different energies in my home, it sometimes feels a bit scary. So, I like to take matters into my own hands – whether a space feels eerie or not – and cleanse my home, using a stick of nag champa incense. I've been doing this for about 15 years. The more popular choice for home cleansing is a stick of sage, but I don't always like the smell, so I use incense instead.

When I moved from London to Somerset, our new house had been derelict for some years. It was dark, decrepit and an awful smell lingered. As time went on and we began to clean, clear and paint the property, I went around each room with a stick of incense, wafting the smoke into each corner and swirling it into cupboards and cubbyholes as I asked that we be welcomed into our new home.

When I went up to the attic, which perhaps felt creepier than the rest of the house and was a space that hadn't yet been properly renovated, I asked old spirits to leave to make space for new. As soon as these words left my lips, I took a step forward on to a rusty nail. It felt like a bad omen. So I decided to keep cleansing that room every day for a week and, by the time we had our first guests come and stay, the home felt safe, positive and cleansed.

If you move into a new home, or have a visit from someone who has a lot of negative energy, you can either use a sage wand to 'smudge' – which means wafting the smoke around the rooms, as I've described above – or use incense, which is thought to welcome good energies. What you choose will depend on the scent that you are most comfortable with. You can try both and see what works for you, but your home will continue to smell of either sage or nag champa for a few hours after, so make sure you like the scent. How does this link to your working life? Well, when you feel happy, safe and comfortable in your home, you sleep better and wake up feeling more positive, which – as I've explained above – feeds into your working day.

After all that cleansing, you know what happened in my new house? After months of watching and waiting for a beautiful yet stubborn magnolia tree in the garden to flower, it started to bloom. It felt rather magical.

SQ tips for spiritualizing your home
Freshen the air

In Germany, there is a practice called *Stosslüften*, which means "shock ventilation". Once or twice a day, all the windows in the home are opened wide to allow stale air out and fresh air in. I love doing this. Even in the depths of winter, it can feel rather refreshing to encourage air circulation around the home, particularly following a bout of illness.

Sage-smudge

Once you've freshened the air, you can keep the windows open while you do a sage-smudge. Ideally, you'll grow your own – or buy locally grown – sage. You can also use pine, rosemary or thyme, depending on what's available in your local area. Light the bundle of herbs and allow the smoke to waft around the room, right into the corners and into any cupboards or shelf space.

Gemstones on windowsills

During the pandemic, I learned that green quartz protects from illness, so I bought pieces to place on all the windowsills in my home. Every so often, I'll gather the stones, cleanse them under the full moon, in bright sunshine or in warm salt water, then let them dry before placing them back on the windowsill.

Room spray

Choose a room spray with essential oils (I love lavender, rosemary and rose) and spritz the air throughout your home after hoovering. Many supermarkets sell a good range, or you can go to a local gift shop and see if they stock independent brands. It feels like your home is getting a full cleanse when it's not only cleaned and cleared but also spritzed with a heavenly scent.

Bring nature indoors

As to whether we should be cutting flowers and sticking them in a vase until they wilt, well, that's up to the individual. But potted plants are a great way to satisfy our biological desire to be closer to nature. In fact, there are proven mental health benefits to having plants in the home, including reduced anxiety. Plus, nurturing and caring for plants can reduce stress levels and boost our mood.[23]

Light candles

Having candles on the table creates a calming focal point while eating. I light a candle at the beginning of every meal I share with my children and it seems to instantly calm them, as well as signalling that it's now time to sit still and eat. After dinner, when we are all finished, they get to blow out the candles and make a wish.

Quiet corner

Choose a space in your home that can be dedicated to thinking, stillness and peace. If you live with other people – including children – tell them that, when you are in the quiet corner, you'd like to be left alone. You can add some cushions to make it

---

[23] "Plants to help ease the mind", thrive.org.uk

comfortable and leave a book to read there, or something to hold while you meditate.

To recap on this chapter, your daily SQ working routine might include:

- Choose to get out on the right side of bed.
- Create an affirmation linked to your intention for the day.
- Repeat the affirmation while walking in nature, or stretching. Really sink into and believe the words as you say them.
- Light a candle or scent diffuser on waking, if you like a slower start.
- Charge your gemstones while you wash.
- At your desk, engage in some happiness journaling.
- Light some incense, using a scent that makes you feel happy, calm and productive.
- If your energy dips, rolls your gemstones in your palm, like worry beads.
- Go for a walk and ask the fairies to help you with your work challenge.
- Sniff something lovely – a candle, or bath salts – for a mindful moment.
- Clear negative energies from your work space, visualizing them as you waft incense around the room and ask them to leave.
- After you've cleared away dinner, light a candle and give thanks for the day that has passed.
- Make a wish, while blowing the candle out.
- Go to bed before all your energy has disappeared and engage in gratitude journaling.
- Set your intention for the following day.

MY SQ JOURNEY

Suzy Ashworth, successful manifestation coach, mentor and creator of Infinite Receiving.

I wasn't raised in a spiritual home, but I did ask to be christened when I was eight, which is a little bit of a weird thing for a child to ask. I was fostered at the age of three months old and my foster parents weren't religious, but my biological mother – who I did see up until I was eight – is a Christian in the Pentecostal church. Occasionally, when I went to see her, I'd be taken to church and there'd be a gospel choir and all of that. So I think that exposure, although it was limited, was probably my first introduction to Jesus.

But my foster parents, who I call Mum and Dad, were not into God, the church or spirituality at all. I don't know why I wanted to be christened, but I always felt I had a connection to something bigger than myself. I remember, after I stopped seeing my natural parents, that I felt I was very blessed to have two sets of parents. Again, that way of thinking, at that age, on reflection feels quite an unusual way to be interacting with the world. But I remember, very distinctly, sitting on the side of my bed thinking I was very lucky.

I was speaking to my spiritual mentor recently about "hope". I'd been listening to some podcasts and feeling quite depressed about the talk of hurtling towards Armageddon and I was thinking: Am I living in a dream world? What my mentor reflected to me was: "This is just an invitation for you to reclaim your relationship to hope. And also get very clear on your purpose, your role: what you are here to do at this time?"

I need to be very centred in my light to see my clients' light. And when there's so much chaos all around – people are so much in their shadow and there's fear, pain and suffering around – for you to be able to be that beacon of light is absolutely imperative.

The biggest opening for me, though, in terms of my spirituality, was when my foster mother died. I was 19. That was pivotal because, when she died, I wasn't there to support her. I was being a typical teenager who had a challenging situation and didn't know how to deal with it . . . but when she died, I wasn't there, so there was a lot of guilt, shame and grief. I remember choosing to write her a letter – maybe asking for forgiveness – and again, choosing to believe that it was worth me writing a letter; that the letter would have an impact. So there was a sense of believing in an afterlife, though not in the traditional sense of a "heaven", where the intention and energy of that letter could be felt.

That set me on a path. I went to Amsterdam and met up with a friend there who was very into manifestation and the law of attraction. She introduced me to a book called The Celestine Prophecy, *which is all about coincidence and serendipity, and I started exploring it all more.*

SQ in business

Before setting up my first business, The Calm Birth School, I did a hypnotherapy diploma and I started to get interested in how the mind works. When I set up that business, I understood that it was my job to help parents envision what it was they wanted to create during their birth. From them telling me what their vision was, I would help them release their fears through tools that would support the vision, such as meditation, mindfulness and creative visualization. I was using those tools, not necessarily from a spiritual place, to build my business.

It was when I launched my second business that I was introduced to Dr Joe Dispenza – the bestselling author, researcher and international lecturer – and went from thinking, This is all in my mind, to learning from Joe Dispenza about the quantum field and infinite possibilities. And it brought me back to the idea there's something bigger, there's something universal: there's a universal intelligence. There are an infinite number of solutions to every problem and your job is to be able to connect with that infinite intelligence. Some people call it "Source", or "the Universe" or "God".

When I set up my second business, I took a course in which one of the pivotal questions asked of us was: "Do you feel supported?" And I broke down in tears because, up until that point, I'd walked around with the weight of the world on my shoulders. I was smiling and happy, but I thought: If I don't do it, it won't get done. I felt as though I was carrying everything for everyone. I had an awakening, in that moment, a realization that, every single step of my life, I had been guided and I had been supported. At that point, my foster father had passed away as well and it was as though there was the energy of my foster father and foster mother, both saying: "She's here, she's awake, she gets it, she's not on her own." I then read Dying to be Me, by Anita Moorjani, in which she talks about her experience of nearly dying and being in the transitional state. Those two things changed the way I interacted with the world.

I allowed myself to be supported on a practical level and then consciously tuned into the support that I believe is always available to us. That's when I started practising meditation from a place of, "Let's get quiet and we can connect," rather than, "Let's try and manifest something." It was more about a connection with Source and my inner guidance, inner wisdom, inner essence.

Mindset will get you very far, but it's when you go beyond the mind that you realize your mind's a problem-solving machine. It works based on the experiences you have seen, heard, touched or tasted. Those experiences might also be gleaned from something on TV, or from your parents, but your mind is all based on experience. The reality is that completely relying only on yourself is a very narrow and limited perspective from which to try and solve all your problems. The bringing together of minds, however, is so powerful.

Later in my career, I undertook a retreat called Quantum Healing. I went to Costa Rica for ten days to become a certified quantum healer. I read the sales page, didn't know what they were talking about – it was like a different language – but, energetically, I knew I had to be there. So I went and they got us to do all these very weird exercises, so beyond the mainstream. Even though my mind didn't understand half the things we did and I don't necessarily use any of the tools from that certification, something happened in that space. I became aware of a big wild world beyond my mind, and that, if I tried to use my mind to work it out, I was never going to be able to do so. That's the quantum field.

Since going on that retreat, I have tried to go beyond my mind many times. Sometimes it's very scary, sometimes magical, sometimes amazing. But the lessons I've learned when I'm not in my right mind have been absolutely pivotal for me.

My SQ toolkit

Plant medicine has been most powerful for me. Ayahuasca (a tea made from the leaves of the Psychotria viridis shrub and the stalks of the Banisteriopsis caapi vine) and bufo (venom from the Bufo alvarius toad that has been collected and dried). Though I wouldn't recommend that everyone does bufo, it was quite significant for me in terms of my spiritual connection.

I have **crystals** all around the house and, energetically, they change the energy, change how busy my mind is. You can use crystals to channel certain things. But I don't need a crystal to connect with Source, I'm always connected to Source.

I have a special tool called an **ankh**. It was bought for me as a celebration when my business crossed seven figures. The stones *in it are all coded energetically to me. There's amethyst and agate. It's very good when you're meditating. I put it on my chest and it works to open up my channel more.*

*A **palo santo wand with crystals** at each end. When meditating, or in ceremony, I use this. It acts as an amplifier. When you touch these crystals, you feel their vibration; they feel very magical.*

*I have a **Stargate wand** too. My mentor opened up the portal for the Stargate energetically and then you can set your intentions; when you're meditating, it's supposed to amplify the intention. I have an intention to create an eight-figure business, for sure, but my intentions are largely around who I want to be, such as: Can my heart be more open? How do I become of greater service? What do I release in order to step into the frequency of creating eight-figure impact? I meditate on these intentions.*

SQ books I'd recommend

Quantum Warrior: The future of the mind *by John Kehoe*
Breaking the Habit of Being Yourself: How to lose your mind and create a new one *by Dr Joe Dispenza*
Letting Go: The pathway of surrender *by David R Hawkins*

Cacao ceremonies for networking

Do you find networking dry and exhausting? You're not alone. So how about shaking things up and hosting a cacao ceremony for founders or freelancers in your area? Forget name badges and small talk, it's all about going deep. These ceremonies can provide the perfect networking backdrop for businesspeople who crave – and need – something more.

Here, Samantha Hadadi – women's health and hormone coach, photographer and content creator – shares her tips for running your own cacao ceremony.

What are cacao ceremonies?

Cacao ceremonies have been practised for centuries, rooted in Mayan and Ancient Aztec culture. Shamans were also believed to hold ceremonies to help prepare them for awakening and guidance. They have seen a resurgence over the last few years, due, perhaps, to the pressures of our lives and an ever-growing need to escape. After all, what could be more soothing than settling down with a steaming mug of silky smooth, rich and indulgent cacao?

Cacao ceremonies are just as they sound: a celebration of cacao, ritualizing it and turning it into an act of self-care. They are designed to harness the healing, medicinal qualities of cacao (known to be rich in antioxidants, as well as calming magnesium – a crucial nutrient when it comes to relaxing) – packaging it up into a loving, spiritual practice.

And while these ceremonies are ideal to try on your own, they are also perfect as an alternative networking event, creating a powerful way to connect with others in a group setting.

What are the benefits?

Cacao ceremonies help us to connect to our heart space. The more we do this, the more we are able to sweep our gaze over areas of our lives or businesses with new-found clarity, wisdom and even intuition. When we slip into a heart-centred space, we are also able to connect with others more deeply, making these ceremonies the perfect practice for today's modern businesswoman. What's more, the cacao from the ceremony also provides the body with a natural caffeine boost – no espresso shot needed – making it ideal for breakfast or morning events.

What do I need?

To host your own cacao ceremony at networking events, you'll need a designated sacred space – this can simply be a quiet, peaceful and comfortable room – and access to hot water. You may also like to arrange notebooks and pens around the room for jotting down any wisdom or guidance that pops up during the ceremony. Finally, you'll need to purchase some ceremonial-grade cacao, or you could try simple cacao powder for a more accessible option.

How to hold a cacao ceremony

Set up your space. To host a ceremony, start by ensuring your space is calm, clean and peaceful. How you'd like to do this depends on you and the people you'll be networking with. You might like to dot cosy blankets and candles around the room, pop on a playlist of healing music, burn some incense, or even arrange crystals of your choice around the space. The choice is entirely your own.

Then, make the cacao in the following way:

Healing Cacao Elixir

Serves 1

20–40g (¾–1½oz) ceremonial-grade block of cacao
    (start small if you're not used to cacao), or you can
    also use powder
240ml (1 cup) water
½ tsp ground cinnamon
pinch each of salt and cayenne pepper
drop of vanilla extract
sweetener of choice, to taste, such as maple syrup,
    coconut sugar or honey

Chop the block of cacao as finely as possible. Gently warm the water – taking care not to boil it – then whisk with all the remaining ingredients. Alternatively, blend until frothy and creamy and the cacao has dissolved.

Let go.

As you hug your cacao close to your heart, guide the group in relaxing their bodies and connecting with the breath. Breathe deeply, in through the nose and into the belly. Eyes can be closed, or the gaze can be softened. Simply relax and let it all go.

Gratitude

Next, it's important to share or acknowledge what you're grateful for in that moment. This helps you to connect with the heart. It could be a successful meeting, an exciting new venture or contract. The choice is yours.

What's your intention?

Either alone or as a group, set an intention for the ceremony: what is it you'd like this time to help you to achieve? Is it to listen to your inner guidance, for example, or to enable you to connect with others?

As you sip your cacao together, try to take pleasure in the experience. Enjoy the enticing aroma of the chocolate, the richness of the taste, or any of the different flavours you may notice.

When you're ready, close the ceremony. Gently guide everyone's attention back to their breath, encouraging them to repeat their intention from before. As you close the ceremony, jot down any insights or wisdom that may have been received. If it feels appropriate to do so, share these insights together.

See this as a moment for peace, as a moment for sanctuary, as you connect with one another.

4

DESIGN YOUR SHRINE

During one of the school holidays, my husband and I took our three kids on a trip to Devon, in south-west England. We had rented a first-floor flat in an apartment block for the week and, as we entered at street level, the musty smell reminded me of my grandma and grandad's old flat, down the road from where I grew up. It was dark and not very loved. We went upstairs and the hall, living space and bedrooms all had the same brown speckled carpet, laid because it hides stains well, and off-white walls. It was pretty uninspiring. But then we tend to book everything last minute, and it was both available and quite cheap. I felt comforted by the association I had between that flat and my grandparents' flat, which I hadn't visited since they passed away 20 years previously. Also, there was a lovely sea view from the kitchen.

I love beautiful interiors and interesting architecture – and this apartment was not that – but we were there to spend time as a family and there was at least plenty of space for the kids to run around. Also, I was able to go for a run every morning before diving into the cool late-October sea and commune with nature.

Our first night's sleep was bad – the people above threw a party that started at 3am – and we woke feeling a bit grumpy. But after a run, swim in the sea and shower, I was perking up a bit. I then walked into the room where my three kids were sleeping and noticed something rather beautiful. On the bedside table next to my daughter's bed, there was a collection of items: shells she'd found on the local beach, her new teddy bear, some tiny drawings she'd done. And it was all laid out so carefully; she had taken time to display these objects in a way that would be pleasing to her eye and perhaps also – though probably subconsciously – as a form of exhibition for the rest of us. She hadn't told me she was doing it. It felt like she was creating a form of shrine to connect her with both home and the holiday we were on. An homage to normal life, as well as to this exciting trip we'd taken (in spite of the rather uninspiring surroundings, we were all feeling quite giddy to be away together and by the sea).

Having a central space for the objects that you treasure and that hold meaning for you can feel comforting. A space that you return to, either while you're travelling away from home, as my daughter did, or when you're working. It can provide a feeling of safety and sanctuary, especially when you assign a particular meaning to the objects you have included.

Traditionally, shrines create a physical space for people of various religions to honour a god, or deity.

As noted in an online encyclopaedia: "One of the distinctive features of religion is that its objects do not 'exist' in the ordinary sense of the word. Deity, spirit, soul, afterlife and other familiar categories of religion lie outside the realms of everyday objects in time and space. However, human beings across multiple cultures experience the presence of these religious realities at particular times and places and in relation to material objects."[24]

And so, in the absence of a physical person or "being" to pray to – or to bow in front of – people create a shrine. As the same online encyclopaedia goes on to say, "Much of the work

---

[24] "Shrines", encyclopedia.com, 23 February 2023

of shrines is to provide habitations for sacred presences within the everyday world. As places having a particular shape and materiality, shrines give particular density to complex sets of religious associations, memories, moods, expectations and communities. Shrines may be seen as sites of condensation of more dispersed religious realities, places where meanings take on specific, tangible and tactile presence."

I first came across memorable shrines travelling around Thailand and India in my late teens. Growing up in London, I don't remember seeing any. But there I was, in south-east Asia, walking past dozens of shrines every day. In Thailand, they create *san phra phum*, meaning "spirit houses", small temple-like structures placed in front of people's homes, often only the size of a small doll's house. There is a Buddhist belief that these spirit houses protect the energies of the home and the people living there. There will often be offerings on and around the spirit house, such as fruit, flower garlands, incense, candles and small religious statues.

"Guardian spirits are everywhere, whether near houses, temples, farmlands or rivers. They protect different places and look after us," Narongdet Sapprathueang, a spiritual adviser, has said.[25] "It is believed that appeasing the spirits facilitates happiness, prosperity and a peaceful life." A Brahman priest or Buddhist monk might come to show a homeowner where to place the spirit house, to ensure the spirits are at peace. Next, a pit will be dug for it and money is sometimes laid in the pit. When deciding its position, it's important that the spirit house never falls under the shadow of the house.

When I arrived in what would become my new home in Somerset, there were Buddhist statues made of stone dotted

[25] "Thai 'spirit houses' believed to bring fortune", Emmy Sasipornkarn, dw.com, 1 September 2021

around the front garden, as well as lots of stone cats and a dog. I could sense that the previous owner – now deceased – had placed meaning on these objects; they mattered to her. And it felt wrong to remove them. Everything inside the home had been removed by professional home-clearers before we moved in, so I couldn't hold on to anything from inside except a box of letters she had written to her dad, but I have kept the stone monuments . . . perhaps in an act of superstition.

My instant connection to these statues, and feeling that I shouldn't shake things up by disturbing them or throwing them away, reminded me of the power of certain objects. Or the power we might place on them, anyway. And this is what a shrine is made from: a collection of objects that carry meaning, gathered together as a central focus for prayer, meditation or magic spells.

In India, there are public shrines that people visit for a particular reason. For instance, the "visa" temple in Hyderabad, the capital of southern India's Telangana state. This is one of the oldest shrines in the area and devotees head there in the hope that a visit will help them to get their visa approved. They go there and pray, perform rituals and promise to complete further rituals.[26] There are also roadside, or personal, shrines around parts of India, dedicated to Hindu deities or Muslim saints, depending on the region. In the south of India, there are also Buddhist and Christian shrines. In a research paper on wayside shrines[27], Professor Ghassem-Fachandi describes the emergence of roadside shrines in the city of Ahmedabad

---

[26] "Out-of-the-ordinary shrines in India and their secrets", Panchali Dey, timesofindia.indiatimes.com, 10 August 2017

[27] "Introduction. Wayside Shrines in India: An Everyday Defiant Religiosity", Borayin Larios and Raphaël Voix, *South Asia Multidisciplinary Academic Journal*, vol. 18, 2018

as a "mushrooming" phenomenon. He believes: "The success of the structure is predicated on the creative ability to attract the fleeting residents into short-lived economic and spiritual transactions during their daily travel routine to work and back home."

It's hard to imagine having these shrines outside of our homes in the west. But I think we ought to consider bringing them into the general culture. These small structures are built and carefully displayed to protect us and the spirits in and around our homes. But they are also an offering to people passing by, a place where they can stop for a moment and pray, or just slow down during what might otherwise be a busy working day.

If we don't have shrines outside our homes, or alongside them, we can set them up within our homes. They can be a sacred space for your own prayer, thoughts and mindful meditation, or the place where you cast magic spells for work success (for more on this, see page 225).

My shrine is on my work desk. I have:

- A **scented candle** that I light as soon as I sit down to work. I enjoy the ritual of lighting it with matches: striking the match, waiting for the wick to catch the fire, watching the flame grow. It requires patience. And I say a wish at the end of the day, as I blow it out.
- A **Tibetan singing bowl** to "dong" at the beginning of the day, and again at the end. I often say something, out loud, while drumming the side of the bowl, such as: "I look forward to an amazing working day." And then, as I finish for the day, I might say: "Thank you for this working day and all that I achieved."
- My **scent diffuser**. I add in some drops of oil, choosing between those intended to make you happy, boost your energy or de-stress, depending on what I need. Once it's on

and the steam is shooting out, it feels like the air is being filled with goodness.

- I have a pot of **incense** and I'll pull out a stick to light and waft around if I need a moment of calm, something to focus on away from my screen, or to clear away bad energies and vibes if I'm feeling frustrated. There's also a small brown ceramic bowl to rest the incense stick, while it burns out.

- There's a pot of **gemstones**, filled to the brim. I'll tip out a handful to hold while saying a magic spell, prayer or incantation. Often, I'll check the meaning of the gemstones that have landed in my hand, to see if they are giving me something I didn't know I needed (love, strength, hope and so on).

- I have a **small wooden elephant** from India that reminds me of travel, adventures and the spiritual experiences I had while travelling around Asia. Also, I believe the elephant symbolises strength, courage and striding ahead confidently. Glancing at it makes me feel similarly strong and courageous.

- A **tiny ceramic model of a woman** who looks like a milkmaid. My mum gave her to my daughter and said she'd bring good luck when she was starting a new school. I now have her with me for luck (and to keep her from getting lost in my children's bedroom). Though my daughter sometimes takes her back.

- A **pot of pens**. This might seem like an obvious thing to have on your desk, but I made the pot, so it feels special. The pens hold more meaning to me than they might to someone else, as I'm a writer. They are symbolic of my career dreams, love of writing and need to communicate.

- A **glass vase with beautiful dried flowers** that a lovely friend bought for me when I moved into my new house. She didn't know that she was buying them from another lovely friend of mine, who is a flower farmer. So the dried flowers represent female friendship, coming together and beauty.

- My **tarot card deck and booklet** explaining what each card means. I regularly consult these cards if I'm feeling unsure about a work opportunity or a more personal matter. They guide me towards the answer that I know deep inside but can't yet see.
- I have one of **my poems**, framed, with flowers that I dried pressed on to the paper. This represents my creativity and connection to nature and it serves as a link to where I now live, because the flowers were grown locally. The poem is about tender, early motherhood and the love I have for my children.
- A beautiful **balm with lavender and rosemary**. I dip my index finger in and rub it on my temples if I'm feeling a bit anxious or stressed and it instantly calms me.

My work desk shrine – and shrines in general – create a central focal point for your spiritual work. It's a space where you can sit and have a meditative moment, while reciting magic spells or affirmations and holding a gemstone in your hand. It's a space where body, mind and spirit can all connect. You can go to your shrine if you need a confidence boost, a moment of calm, or a place from which to manifest.

In my shrine, little statues and ornaments will come and go, depending on how I'm feeling. I'll pick up something new (though usually second-hand) to add to my collection and, sometimes, things go missing. I see the transition of these objects as I see life: our needs change over time and nothing is permanent. Often, when I first sit down at my desk in the morning, I'll arrange and re-arrange the objects until they look pleasing. And then, observing the arrangement, I move into a meditative state, observing each individual object. I look to them for questions and answers. And I use them throughout the day.

Travel shrine

When my sister, Lauren, was going into hospital to give birth to her first baby, she took along the usual essentials: nightwear for her, nappies and newborn baby clothes, toothbrush, cosmetics. But she also took a bunch of items that she could set up as a form of shrine on her bedside table. She chose those that would bring her comfort, familiarity and hope while she laboured.

She took: a room diffuser with lavender aromatherapy oil and a dimmable light; a weighted lavender shoulder pad (that you heat in the microwave); a maternity massage oil; and tropical juice. I love this combination of objects that appeal to different senses and would also ground Lauren during a potentially wild time in childbirth. In fact, these items both ground and transport you. They can bring you down to a place of calm if you feel your cortisol levels rising, but a sniff of lavender oil in the air, the smell and touch of a lavender pad, or the zingy taste of tropical fruit juice can also take you somewhere else, in body and mind, for a moment's escape.

Having some carefully chosen objects with you when you travel can also bring you comfort and familiarity. Let's say you're travelling alone for work and have a meeting or conference that you feel nervous about. If you set up your shrine on a desk, dressing table or next to the bed, you can use each of the objects you've chosen to help you to feel focused on the event you have coming up, while also rooted to your home. You might like to shrink down the shrine and take just three items, if you're tight on suitcase space. That might be: one to hold (a gemstone or small ornament); one to smell (a scented candle, it doesn't have to be lit, or incense); and one to gaze at while you set an intention for the outcome of the trip (such as my "lucky lady" ornament).

On a recent weekend away, I found myself grabbing a small heart charm from my dressing table. I'm not sure who put it there, but it looked like the perfect item to take in my pocket. As I held it in my hand, I thought: *This will be my lucky charm for the weekend; it will ensure that the trains run on time and everything goes as smoothly as possible.* I popped it in my pocket and, later in the day when we were waiting for a train, I said to my daughter: "We don't have to worry, as I brought this lucky charm to make sure the trains come on time." She liked this idea and, even though the train was delayed by a few minutes, we were able to feel upbeat and hopeful, because of the charm and the meaning we'd assigned to it.

As you begin to assign greater meaning to the objects in your shrine, you might find yourself doing the same with objects outside of your home, too. One of my fondest memories of living in London, in the home where I had each of my three babies, was when we were standing by the window one morning. My youngest was obsessed with watching the refuse men emptying the bins, so each Wednesday morning, we'd see the flashing orange lights, hear the groan of the vehicle and rush over to see the bins being tipped and emptied into the lorry. One morning, a man came into our front garden, pulled out the bin and attached it to the arms on the lorry. While waiting for it to be emptied, he returned to our front garden, grabbed a bunch of lavender from our bush, crushed it between his gloves and lifted his hands to his nose to smell the aroma he'd released. He looked gleeful as he inhaled the calming lavender scent. He then looked at us, smiled, waved goodbye and went on his way.

This was an example of a spiritual moment with nature and with us. That job – emptying smelly bins – must be hard. And yet, within an otherwise difficult day, he managed to find a moment of joy, peace and communion with nature. An SQ-raising exercise, for sure.

Totems

A totem is an object – such as an animal or plant – that serves as the emblem of a family or clan and often as a reminder of its ancestry. It's usually a carved or painted representation of the object. Back in prehistoric times, reindeer, bison and horses were often depicted – in art work in caves – and it's possible that they were totems to those people. But the word totem is thought to be derived from *doodem*, which comes from the Algonquian-speaking Anishinaabe tribe in North America. It means "my clan" or "my tribe". The symbolic object might be worshipped for bringing protection to the tribe, and the ancestral heritage it embodies.[28]

I love this idea of focusing your vision, energy and belief on a specific object for a sense of belonging, ancestral connection and protection. I see the elephant as my totem. Elephants have a matriarchal head, so an older female elephant leads the herd. And the family of elephants is female-focused: mothers, sisters, daughters. They also have friends and develop strong bonds with them, as well as with blood family members.[29] My connection to women – the maternal line – is strong, and to my daughter and female friends, so my elephant feels like a symbol of that.

For your own totem – an object that you can keep as part of your shrine that will make you feel connected and protected – you could visit a junk shop, car boot sale (yard sale) or charity

[28] "Why Did Prehistoric People Draw in the Caves?" artsandculture.google.com

[29] "Six facts about elephant families", Helena Williams, independent.co.uk, 19 December 2013

(thrift) shop. See if there are any trinkets that catch your eye. Everything has potential meaning, so start with something you like, then look up the more general symbolism online for added spiritual connection. As you place your totem among the other items making up your shrine, you can give thanks for the part this object is playing in your life. "Thank you for protecting me, connecting me and giving me a sense of belonging."

Ten crystals for work success

When investing in your own set of crystals, think about what you would like to use them for. Different crystals hold different energies and can help in various ways. I'm going to share ten crystals you might like to have to help with work success.

Set an intention for something you'd like – more energy, new creative ideas – then hold the relevant stone in your hand. Close your eyes as you hold it and imagine that the crystal is transferring the energy into your body. Absorb it. Feel it rushing through your bloodstream.

And remember that you can supercharge your crystals by cleaning them in bright sunlight, in salt water or under a full moon (see pages 107 and 120). The idea is that you are releasing old energies from the gemstone and returning it to its purest – and most powerful – form.

- Energy: clear quartz
- Motivation: tiger's eye
- Prosperity: sapphire
- Luck: jade
- Creativity: citrine
- Inner strength and growth: moonstone
- Clarity: obsidian
- Groundedness: turquoise
- Ideas: bloodstone
- Intellect: ruby

TECH AND SPIRITUALITY

Bethany Koby is a designer, social entrepreneur, educator and the founder of both Tech Will Save Us and Fam Studio.

My mum's sister was the radical in the family and a really important figure in my life. She was very political, often going on protest marches, then travelled to Tibet and became very spiritual – a practising Zen Buddhist. I was about seven or eight at the time and she played a significant role in how I saw the world. She taught me how to meditate with rice when I was ten. She gave me The Tibetan Book of Living and Dying *and it really influenced me. It contains a depth of philosophy and shows that life is an investigation, a questioning of our purpose and existence that can be framed in many different ways. My dad, a photographer, is very spiritual too in his own way and he brought a lot of philosophical breadth to my world.*

My first real foray into spirituality, though, was yoga, when I was at university. It became a really interesting bodily experience that helped me to feel some of these philosophies I had read about in a way that wasn't so intellectual. It was an embodied way. I was always drawn to friends and experiences that had a spiritual undertone. My husband, although not practising in any significant way, is a spiritual guy. He practises reiki and has learned martial arts for years. His mum is a gemologist with an amazing healing background. I don't think any of this has happened by accident. All these things layer up; they become a web that helps you to make sense of life through these practices: physical, intellectual, meditation.

My whole life, I had a mindfulness practice. I didn't have the language to describe it like that in the earlier days – that vocabulary only came more recently – but there was a mindfulness to how I worked. I'm a designer and I've worked in the creative industries for a long time, and I think some creative practices are mindful in a way.

About four years ago, I took a meditation course and it really changed my understanding of the difference between mindfulness and meditation.

At that time, my longing was for space. Physical space, emotional space, mental space. I run businesses, I have two children, I have a full life and I wanted space. At first, I thought that space needed to happen through going away – leaving – a retreat, maybe. But, through that meditation course, I learned the practical side of it: how to really meditate and to accept the ebb and flow of what meditation practice is. And what I felt was this enormous amount of space. Not space outside, but space inside. And it became probably the most luxurious experience I'd had in years. As a mum, and a woman in the world – I come from a long history of martyrs who've given a lot and made sacrifices – I felt a need for an unapologetic collection of something for myself.

I ran Tech Will Save Us – an ed-tech start-up – for seven years. It was part of a fast-paced start-up world, very masculine, very ambitious. But in that journey, I somehow lost some parts of myself, some of the feminine parts of myself, not intentionally, almost without knowing. I think that's where my need for space came from. I was so available and so immersed in the delivery of this project, or business, that I didn't have space for my own dreams or my own imagination. So starting to really practise meditation in an intentional way helped me to create a healthy separation from work and ambition and creating for output.

Now, I meditate once or twice a day for at least 20 minutes. I've evolved my practice a few times. It's something I can't imagine living without, ever. For years, I used calmness apps – and they were great starting places – however, when I really learned a practice, it was different. I didn't need anything for it. I first did transcendental meditation, which uses mantras. I love the philosophies behind it. There's an intellectual side to meditation that I think is really interesting: the teachings and history behind it, what's actually neurologically happening in your brain while it's in different states. Then there's the physical, embodied state that happens, which is why meditation has lasted for so long. Because it actually works. It delivers outcomes that you can feel and hold on to.

Since then, I've taken a formless meditation workshop, which is interesting because you meditate with your eyes open. You're not staring at anything; you have a soft gaze but you're not closing your eyes, so you're not going inside yourself, you're almost bringing the world into the meditation. I find it very powerful and different.

I have a close circle of entrepreneurs, all evolving our creative and life practices, and I think there's something about growing in a community that feels really important. There's a beautiful quote from the Dalai Lama that the next Buddha will be a "sangha": a community, not an individual. I really believe that. Whatever our questions are right now, somehow community is the answer. It isn't an *individual journey, it's a journey together. Enlightenment will happen together in this next cycle of life. The spiritual narrative has been around gurus and individuals in the past, but that's not what I'm hearing right now.*

Technology and SQ practices

Tech "scaffolding" has made spiritual practices more accessible. That's amazing. There are certain meditation apps I really love, such as Wake Up: I love the curation and sophistication of the content. Tech makes various philosophies way more available. I also listen to podcasts and audiobooks. These don't replace my practice; they are a complement or a supplement to a practice that feeds that intellectual side of a spiritual practice for me. I also listen to Tara Brach's podcast: she's saved me on several occasions. Her podcast has been unbelievably powerful and useful and she gives beautiful sermons and meditations. I've done several. I will go for a walk, listen to her podcast, then do a meditation to solidify the intellectual into the body. These experiences are only possible because of technology. And they are available anywhere, wherever I am.

There are some edgier things happening too, such as Dreamachine. It's a beautiful creative project based on something similar that happened in the 1950s, when an academic and an artist came up with the first version. A group of academics and artists have taken that concept and brought it to a contemporary setting. It's an experience. You walk into an interesting circular space, very well designed, an art work that you experience with your eyes shut. You're wearing a mask and a strobe light is flashing in front of you, with sound, too. It's an academic research project, so it's curated based on how your brainwaves change, how your body responds, and the experience is slightly different for everyone. It essentially replicates things that happen when tribal communities do trance dances, or when you take psilocybin (see page 78), or your brain is in any altered state. The strobe experience creates the same type of visual waves on the inside of your eyes. At first I was scared by the experience, as it was quite intense. But then I just smiled for about 30 minutes. When you leave the space, there's a table with chalk where you can draw what you saw. You're sitting with a bunch of strangers drawing these psychedelic experiences you had and talking to each other. It is a beautiful, spiritual experience. So technology can play a role in bringing us to altered states, though it's not really understood how and why we want to have these altered states.

On a base level, technology disseminates content and widens access, but there's actually a way more substantial and interesting role it can play in simulating, supporting and scaffolding spiritual experiences.

The tech industry

There's something emerging around tech, especially in San Francisco, where a lot of these very old methodologies have become commodified. I remember going to San Francisco and everyone working in tech was doing ayahuasca retreats, or weekend retreats where they'd purge, then go back to their job and make loads of cash.

But people are longing for a different way of being in the world and I think something new is emerging around that. My friends who are into astrology and deep wisdom *would say: "This is on the cards; this is the era of the feminine, this is what the world needs right now and this is what's emerging."*

I heard the most beautiful definition of spirituality recently. The teacher said that "spirituality" – the word itself – worries people, because it's often associated with some kind of religion or dogma or things that make it feel as though it's not yours. And he said that, if we looked at spirituality as a way of connecting to the world and each other, and not connected to a dogma or religion – which is really what it is – everyone would think they were spiritual. Everyone would say, "Of course I have a spiritual practice," because everyone wants to have a relationship to the world and to each other. The word "spirituality" itself has all this baggage – we might picture gurus sitting on a mountain, and that's fine, if that's the choice you make or the path you choose – but spirituality is actually a plural of so many different practices and philosophies. It's a field, really.

The next generation will have technology interweave in their lives differently than it has done for us. We were the generation where apps helped us connect to meditation or mindfulness. Their access to spirit will be way more complex and deep. Their tools will be so much more immersive, rather than that transactional thing where you get wrapped up in an app and win points telling you you're doing well. Dreamachine was embodied, it was time, it was reflection, it was visual, creative, experiential. For me, that's how technology creates connection to spirit, rather than through game-ifying an experience and motivating you through dopamine hits that make you feel addicted to something . . . which is where tech, unfortunately, is at the moment.

There's also the question of access: not everyone has the resources to go to the Amazon. So we are exploring the role technology can play in providing access to spirit-based experiences.

There's lots of interesting research happening in terms of plant-based medicines and the role tech plays in connecting you to spiritual experiences. And, as we know, context is so important. You can do mushrooms with friends in a club when you're 17 and have a very specific kind of experience. Or you can do assisted micro-dosing in a community with chanting and dancing and have a totally different type of experience, because context and environment matter. There's really interesting research happening now, lots of it being funded by humungous tech companies, around the role technology plays in contextualizing ideas and creating safe, immersive experiences that support a spiritual journey.

MY SQ JOURNEY

Yvadney Davis, kids' fashion stylist and award-winning portrait artist.

My SQ upbringing

I was sent to Sunday school at a local church by my mum – I think it gave her some respite – and I really enjoyed learning basic Bible stories. It was a very vibrant Caribbean Pentecostal church, so I loved singing in the choir and that whole upbringing. Mum and I used to listen to gospel music on the radio every week and, while home wasn't super-super-spiritual, I definitely grew up believing in God.

I had lots of questions about the Christian faith when I became a teenager. They weren't answered and I stopped going to church for about ten years. But I was still definitely spiritual. I think this is because I've always been a bit of a "seer". I've had prophetic dreams about people since childhood and was always very much aware that there is more to life than what we see. I knew there was somebody looking out for me and guiding me and giving me comfort. So, even though I stopped going to church, I would still pray. And I still believed there was more to life than what we have.

I found my spirituality again as a young adult. I was invited to a church service and found myself, halfway through, completely overwhelmed with emotion. I couldn't stop crying and I decided to start going to church again. There was nothing bad in my life, I had no problems, a great career, things were all popping. There is no sad story that I needed fixing from . . . I just found that, as I started going back to church and understanding the Bible and the teachings of Jesus in a new way, I felt whole. And a lot of the questions I had, I found answers for, and the questions I didn't find answers for, I made peace with.

Spirituality, for me, means seeing something more. It is the meaning of life, the fact that we are all interconnected and woven together. Woven together as humans, as nature, as the big Universe. Woven together in terms of time, the present and future. Spirituality anchors me. It's a source that empowers me and gives me strength and peace and wisdom.

I don't believe you need to be Christian to be compassionate, but, for me, my faith gives me a sense of wholeness. It gives me some discipline as well. I'm not looking at what other people are doing, but I'm looking at myself and knowing when I need to call myself out: when I may have been impatient with other people, or myself: not giving myself grace. And it gives me a standard of expectation for how I live my life, how I see my future, how I see my responsibilities to my loved ones and also the people around me, and the legacy I want to leave behind.

Increasingly, spirituality helps me to tap into – and understand – my gifts for both "seeing" and for assigning prophetic words to people. I'm able to use that in my business, to see and understand what people need, whether that's in the workplace, making space for them, or with my art.

With my art, one of the things I discovered, when I started taking commissions, was that when I was painting people I was suddenly feeling their emotions, feeling what they needed. For one person, I saw she wanted to feel like a goddess. For another, I felt incredibly sad, really low. During another session – painting the portrait of a mother whose daughter had commissioned me – I couldn't stop laughing; there was so much joy.

The woman I saw who wanted to feel like a goddess, when she messaged me, said: "Goodness, every time I look at this painting, I'm reminded that I'm a goddess." For the person I felt sad about, I was praying into his life while I painted – praying for more peace, more emotional joy, release from that sense of depression – and he said afterwards: "I was feeling really low when you were painting this and it reminds me where I've come from. I'm not that person anymore." When I gave the lady the portrait of her mother, who had passed away after the commission, she was crying tears of joy and said she felt the grief she had carried for so long was really spoken to. She felt that joy that I felt coming from her mum and some sort of peace.

I feel I've been given a mandate, with my art, not only to bring people joy when they see it, or for them to connect with the art, but that there's something spiritually that I'm able to tap into, in people's lives, with my art and with my brushstrokes; giving them blessings.

My daily SQ routine

*I wake up each morning and **give thanks** for the day. I speak goodness into my day.*

*I love **affirmations** that I can listen to and repeat (I find them on YouTube or Spotify). They start my day on a positive note.*

*I give lots of **kisses and tactile hugs** to my children, so that the day feels really positive.*

*In my prayer time, I do **"breath prayers"**. Rather than saying a really long prayer, I just breathe out and give thanks, or say: "This is beautiful," or "Please protect me," or "I love you." Quick prayers, under my breath, as I walk around.*

*I take time to look at **nature**. I'm in awe of creation. It's beautiful. I could get lost in how a bird pecks away at things, how trees move, or how people smile. I'm reminded by those small things just how good life can be. In those moments, I say a prayer.*

How SQ has led to my success

Spirituality has helped me to feel grounded and it's helped, too, in terms of having vision. It's guided me in having wisdom in how I am, as a stylist. It's helped me to build a reputation for keeping up a level of excellence, but also for being honest and open. I love people and I think that's evident in the work I do.

When you're self-employed, there are highs and lows – times when you're rejected, times when you're blessed and overwhelmed with work – and in all of those times, I'm able to step back and not get caught up in either feeling rejected or feeling cocky. Just staying rooted in something bigger than my career. Also, being able to express gratitude for it and not see it as the be-all and end-all.

My faith makes me generous. I believe that it's important to make space for people, for community and for rising up together. In my job as a stylist, I don't like closing doors on people. I like opening doors, bringing people in and helping them to succeed and find their own path. I'm friendly with other kids' stylists: we work as a team and look out for each other.

SQ toolkit

Vision boards. I love them, I'm obsessed. I have a physical vision board, then I have another as a screensaver on my phone. I've done them for friends as well. I make them digital ones to carry around with them. I'm an artist and stylist and I'm very visual, so I like to have a constant visual reminder of things that are of value.

SQ books I'd recommend

Goodbye 2022, Hello 2023: Design a life you love this year *by Project Love*

I love the theory of welcoming the new year and saying farewell to the last one. I'm not keen on the word "manifesting", but this book is about taking stock of where you've been and setting yourself up for another year. Project Love have been producing the books for a few years and I get it every year and buy it for friends, too.

The Gifts of Imperfection *by Brené Brown*
I love Brené Brown, she's amazing. This book is so good for doing some self-reflection and showing myself some grace. I recommend it to everyone, to take stock of who they are. My husband is reading it at the moment. We have to show other people compassion, but also show ourselves compassion.
The Artist's Way: A spiritual path to higher creativity *by Julia Cameron*
This is a spiritual book. Anyone with any spiritual belief system will really enjoy it. I believe creativity is an innate gift from the Universe that we're here to share in many ways – whether it's through your voice, writing, art or fashion. When we're able to amplify our creativity, tap into it and explore it more, it's great for us and for the greater good. Also, each day, this book encourages you to go out and have time by yourself: go to an exhibition, or take a walk in the woods.

SQ in the world
Actors on SQ

For actors, SQ can help them access a deeper meaning in their work.

"Energy can't be created or destroyed, and energy flows. It must be in a direction, with some kind of internal, emotive, spiritual direction. It must have some effect somewhere."[30]

Keanu Reeves

"I don't know if there's a name for that – religion or faith – just that there's something greater than all of us, and it's uniting and beautiful."[31]

Angelina Jolie

"Take care of your inner, spiritual beauty. That will reflect in your face."

Dolores del Rio

"It's the most important part of my life. I don't try to push it on anybody and I don't try to hide it."[32]

Mark Wahlberg

"I always knew that, in order to play Dr King, I had to have God flow through me because when you see Dr King giving those speeches, you see that he is moving in his anointing."[33]

David Oyelowo, on playing Martin Luther King Jr in *Selma*

[30] "Life in hell for Keanu Reeves", today.com, 15 February 2005
[31] "Angelina Jolie on Faith: 'We're Not Alone in the World'", Tara Fowler, people.com, 30 December 2014
[32] "Mark Wahlberg on Family, Faith, and the Importance of Legos", Erin Hill, parade.com, 14 December 2013
[33] "*Selma*'s David Oyelowo on playing MLK and what it means to be Christian", Jim Wallis, sojo.net, 8 January 2015

5

SUPERSTITION AND INTUITION

When I was about 13 – back in the 1990s – I watched *The Craft*, an American film about four witches. I loved it; I loved the four teenagers practising witchcraft, creating spells for good and also to seek revenge on people who'd done them wrong. I was never into the latter, but I certainly liked the idea of using magic for good.

I'm pretty sure it was around this time that my friends and I started "levitating" at sleepovers. One of us would lie on the floor and four others would kneel – two on each side – tapping the body of the person lying down and reciting: "Light as a feather, stiff as a board; light as a feather, stiff as a board." We'd say this over and over again and then, counting down from three, we'd lift the person by holding them under their middle, using just our index and middle fingers that we'd been using to tap. The person's body would, somehow, be "light as a feather" and "stiff as a board". It's actually quite bonkers, thinking back to this. It was proper magic.

Something else we got into was holding seances, to connect with the spirit world. We'd sit in a circle, with an empty glass in the middle and two sheets of paper, one saying "yes" and one saying "no". All members of the seance would place one finger on the glass and we'd call the spirits in. We'd then ask a question (probably something very important to our 13-year-old selves, such as: "Does Jamie fancy Emily?") and we'd see which answer the spirits guided us to. The glass always moved; everyone always denied that they'd moved it. Who knows whether it was someone in the group or the spirits? We got excited by it.

These early forays into magic and spirituality opened up my mind to what might be beyond. It was fun, playful and curious. And for anyone who is right at the beginning of their SQ journey, that's where I'd recommend starting: at a place that feels exciting and fun, rather than scary or daunting. What I've noticed, as I've grown older, is that when people are spiritually connected, they tend to be more open to connection in general. Also, when we feel we are having – or have had – spiritual experiences, it can be a good source of conversation.

I had a great experience a few months after I'd moved into my new house. It's old and was pretty haunted, so I called a friend, Chloe, who uses Shamanic practices to do space clearing (to ask old spirits to leave and make space for the new owners of a home). She came round with a bag of SQ tools – wands, candles, incense, sage – and set it up on a tray. Just before starting, she said: "You've got builders outside working on your kitchen. You might want to give them a heads-up about me being here, because if they hear me chanting and making loud noises, they might wonder what's happening."

So I went out to talk with one of the builders working with my husband and said: "I'm not sure where you sit with these kind of things, but I'm about to have a house clearing and you might hear some strange noises." I prepared myself for comments on how wacky it is. But the builder told me he used to sit as a medium and channel spirits. His mum did, too. And he told me his wife, who is now my friend, had spoken with angels.

Chloe was listening to this conversation. Later, we laughed at what had happened. It was such a lovely moment to connect all of us together. And this is what spirituality does: even if we have different beliefs within the scope of what it means to be spiritual, we can connect on a higher level.

When Chloe was at my house, I took her out into the garden. I'd created a slice of wild meadow – in a bid to connect with nature – and I showed her the area where I'd uprooted a bunch of wild poppies from a mound of earth that was going to be removed, relocating them to my meadow area. Only, when they took root, it wasn't poppies that bloomed; it was montbretia. This is one of the national flowers of Ireland, where my grandparents were from. We have a photo of my grandma, who passed away 20 years ago, standing by a hedgerow in Kerry, where she was from, framed by montbretia. I said to Chloe: "I feel this is a message from my grandma, but I don't know what it's about."

I went on to explain how I'd been visited by my grandma once before. It was a few years after she'd died and I was asleep in my bed in Brighton, where I was living. I felt something pushing down on my legs and woke to see my grandma sitting on them. She looked angry, which was scary and strange, as I didn't once see her angry when she was alive; she was the kindest person I'd ever known. "It sounds like she wanted to make herself known," Chloe said. And I pondered on this for a moment. Perhaps now, she was springing up in the garden, as she knew I'd see and feel her presence but it would be less confronting.

> If you don't believe in an afterlife or the spirits of people who've passed staying on in any way, the story above might sound like an odd series of events. However, this chapter is all about signs. And you get to allocate the meaning of all the signs that you pick up on.

I've shared the above story as an example of a sign that I found comforting – my grandma watching over me, reminding me that she is there to love and guide me in spirit – but you can assign whatever meaning feels exciting and comfortable for you.

Superstition and signs

My mum was superstitious when I was growing up. Umbrellas would never be opened in the house, we wouldn't walk under ladders and she was always knocking on wood when talking about something bad but hoping that it wouldn't come true. So if someone was unwell, she would touch wood and say: "He'll be fine soon, touch wood." I, too, avoid walking under ladders, and I touch wood. Though I have been known to open umbrellas in the house.

Now, though, I find myself drawn only to positive superstitions. So whenever I'm googling the symbolism of something, I seek the positive meaning and discard the negative. Often, I find western cultures create a negative association – with the sighting of a dead animal, for instance, which is assigned a grim meaning that makes you want to avoid it – while eastern cultures assign something more encouraging. You can decide for yourself whether you'd like to see the positive, the negative, or a balance of the two. Of course, I'd encourage you to go for the optimistic viewpoint and seek only good.

When my third baby was three months old, he became seriously ill and had to spend time in hospital. As I walked through the ward, between the room we were staying in and the bathroom, I'd say things to myself, such as: "If I get to the next door without seeing a nurse, he'll be okay." Or: "If I hold my breath for 30 seconds, he won't need to stay on the oxygen machine any longer." I shared something about this on social media and one of my followers said I ought to be careful, as it sounded like acute OCD (obsessive compulsive disorder). It was one of the less supportive comments I received during that time. What I was actually doing was finding anything to which I could attach hope. I needed to have hope, faith, belief and focus. As I came up with these words and ideas about what I needed to do to help my child to be okay, it provided a moment's relief, as I truly believed it might help.

I also practised reiki on my baby as he lay on the hospital bed, covered in tubes and with an oxygen machine keeping him alive. It was something I could do to try to help him. I could bring in the only healing I knew, which was reiki. I lay my hands over his body, covering each of the chakras in turn, and I closed my eyes. I imagined that I was drawing out the viruses and restoring him to good health. Thankfully, after eight days, he was better and we were allowed to go home. Who knows what saved him? Certainly the doctors and nurses, but perhaps there was an element of spirit in there, too.

White feathers

A few years ago, I heard that white feathers bring good luck. Until then, I'd never noticed white feathers. Or grey, or black, or brown. I'd walk past them most days, I expect, but I'd pay no attention. However, as soon as I heard of the association between white feathers and good luck, I started to see them everywhere. I wouldn't just see them out the corner of my eye, though, I'd actively seek them out. I'd scour the floor for white feathers. And, every time I saw one, I'd get a feeling of excitement in my belly, because I'd know it meant that something good was going to happen.

Regarding manifesting, I gave an analogy earlier about a car (see page 32): if you know you want a car, and focus hard on it, you'll find a way to make it happen. If you don't know you want a car, you probably won't get one. The same goes with signs and superstitions. You can either ignore all the signs, pay no attention and miss the moment when something lovely happens, or you can focus on that white feather, feel those belly butterflies and look out for something amazing happening. When you move with an energy of excitement and positivity, guess what? More good stuff comes your way. People respond to your energy and want to help you and give you gifts.

I remember when I'd just read *The Secret*, by Rhonda Byrne. I was walking around with a feeling that good stuff was flowing into my life. The truth was: I had hardly any money, was working on the door of a nightclub in London and in a pub (earning very little) and writing articles for free for a local newspaper, trying to break into journalism. I'd been feeling pretty anxious and unsure of my future. But then I decided to welcome in a feeling of things flowing in my direction: opportunities, gifts, love.

I went to a shopping mall in London. I had enough money for one cheap floral jumpsuit, so I took it up to the till to pay for it. When I handed over the jumpsuit, the man behind the till popped it in a plastic bag, handed it over and said: "This one's on us." Now, I'm not sure the store's management would have been down with this person handing me a free jumpsuit, but I am sure that the energy I felt, while believing that good things were coming, was what made that man give me the jumpsuit for free. If I'd walked in with my head hung low, shoulders slumped and frowning because life felt hard, I believe he wouldn't have done that.

I've shared the idea with my children that seeing white feathers will bring good luck. Now, they are obsessed with them too and will often squeal when they spot one, saying: "I wonder what good luck this will bring."

I did recently see a black feather on my doorway and it felt like a bad omen, so I took it in the car with me and threw out the window far from my home. I then went for a run and saw lots of crows and black feathers and it didn't feel very good. But I decided to not pay too much attention to that, as it didn't feel like a positive SQ experience, and instead to keep looking for signs that good things are coming. You get to choose whether you hold on to the "good" or "bad". I not only seek out positive signs and superstitions, but I also switch superstitions that some people see as negative to positive.

Number 13

I have lived at house number 13 a few times and I've loved those homes. So I now say that 13 is my lucky number. If I go to a gym and there's an empty locker that's number 13, I actively use it. I have a friend who lives at number 13, and, when she told me that was her door number, I excitedly said: "That's such a lucky number." She said others had told her it was unlucky and it made her feel bad, so she was pleased to hear this. This is an example of spreading positivity, not fear. We don't need to be sharing negative examples of superstitions, but positive ones can feel exciting.

I also feel excited whenever I see that we're approaching a Friday 13th date in the year ahead. I don't see it as a spooky, Halloween-vibes day, I see it as a special date in the diary. It lifts my spirits and I wish the people around me a happy Friday 13th. We can reframe any superstitions that we like, flipping what others see as dark into something light and hopeful.

Be wary

On that note, when I was younger – in my early twenties – I went for a tarot reading in London. A woman did my reading and, partway through, told me that something terrible was going to happen to someone in my family and it would tear the family apart. She said it would happen in the next five years. I spent the next five years waiting for something terrible to happen . . . but it never did. Fortunately, I've long passed that five-year mark. I had another reading, from a woman in Brighton, and I told her what had been said. She let me know that a reading should never be negative like that, but it should always be positive or hopeful.

So do be wary of anyone who says something to you that feels scary or dark. That is not someone with a high SQ. Or EQ. Or IQ.

Likewise, while experimenting with paying for different spiritual experiences (channelling, clairvoyants, tarot readings or similar), you might find that some really don't resonate with you, or feel like a scam. Sadly, there are people out there making money from pretending to be someone they're not. So be vigilant, go with word-of-mouth recommendations and, if you get an "off" feeling about someone, listen to it: that is your intuition knowing that something isn't quite right or that this person simply isn't the right match for you. I had a very odd EFT (emotional freedom technique) session, where the "therapist" kept talking over me, didn't listen and was telling me what to do about certain personal situations. She certainly wasn't trained as a coach or therapist and shouldn't have been talking to me in this way. At the end of the session, she gave me some flower essence to drink and I felt ill.

Animals

In many cultures, animals hold strong meaning. For instance, in India, you see cows walking around towns and cities and no one will hurt them, as they are considered sacred by Hindus. They were Lord Krishna's favourite animal and serve as a symbol of wealth, strength and abundance[34], so people of the Hindu faith don't eat beef. In Japan, the fox is sacred to those following both Shinto and Zen Buddhism. There are Inari shines, where people go to worship the Inari deity, who is associated with foxes.[35]

We can look to the symbolism attached to animals in the country we are living in, and we can also create our own. Here's an example. Last winter, I'd just moved to Somerset and was living on the edge of the countryside. I'd found it hard making the move, as I was relocating with my family – husband and kids – but leaving behind my parents, siblings and nephews, plus some good friends. One morning, I was out running and there was a mystical-looking mist lying low on the fields. As I ran down my usual dirt track, a narrow path that leads towards a river, I spotted two deer up ahead, leaping gracefully over a fence into the fields. It felt like the most magical sighting. And it made me feel like I was in the right place.

In that moment, I could have seen the deer, appreciated the moment and left it there. Or, do as I did: decide it was a sign from a higher power, that this was where I was supposed to be living right now. That my life would fill up with more magical experiences if I stayed. And it has.

Another sign I had, from an animal – in terms of the resonance

[34] "India's Sacred Cows", *Religion & Ethics Newsweekly*, pbs.org, 27 February 2015

[35] "6 Things to Know About the Inari Fox in Japanese Folklore", David McElhinney, japanobjects.com, 5 February 2022

of "place" – was when I was on holiday one summer. I was out running in the morning and spotted what I thought was a snake crossing my path. I was really scared to see the silver snake slithering ahead of me and I spent some time thinking about what it might mean. I had thought about moving to that place, where I saw the snake, and I took this as a sign that I perhaps shouldn't. Seeing that snake (in reality, a harmless slow worm) helped me to access my subconscious thoughts on what it would be like to move there and decide against it.

I also notice slugs and snails. The first time I had a slug crossing my path when I was out for a run, I looked up the spiritual meaning of slugs. They apparently signify, among other things, a need to slow down; this resonated with me, as I was rushing through life. And so now, when I see a slug, I take it as a sign that I need to slow down, to do less, be more present. I find it really useful.

Also, I learned that spiders represent creativity. So I love seeing spiders around the place, as it makes me feel as though creative opportunities are coming, or that I should get creative myself: make music, write poetry, draw, bake.

But, whenever I'm looking at the spiritual meaning of animals or insects, I gloss right over anything negative and just fixate on the positive. For instance, I found a dead bee trapped in a spider's web in my studio shed space. I was a bit sad, as we don't want to be seeing dead bees. But I decided to look up its spiritual meaning. At first, words came up such as "disease", "death", "losing a loved one". And I panicked. But then I carried on reading and found this explanation . . ."Often feared for their menacing sting, many of us cringe at the sound of the bee's buzz. Although they are less likely to attack until provoked, a dead bee indicates that a threat has passed and fortunate times are set to arrive. A symbol of hope and a guarantee that great things have yet to come, the death of this assertive animal teaches us how to focus on the present and helps us achieve a more peaceful mind."

And this is the meaning I chose to focus on. You see, we always have a choice about whether we want to err on the positive or the negative, to be optimistic or pessimistic. And I choose positive and optimistic whenever I can. I choose to see black cats as positive, for instance. It doesn't really matter whether any good things happen after encounters with these animals or not; what matters is that we are experiencing a moment of excitement and buoyancy, rather than a moment of doom and fear.

We pick dandelion seed heads as a family, as I did as a child, and blow away the fluffy seeds. While doing this, we make a wish. Again, it is a form of superstition, but I welcome any opportunity to make a wish with open arms. It helps me to get clear on what I want, right now, and to believe that I may just get it . . . in this case, with the help of a dandelion.

I had a strange experience recently. I went into my kitchen to butter some crackers for my children and, as I spread the butter with a bone-handled knife handed down from my grandparents to my mum, then from her to me, the blade snapped in half. I wasn't pressing hard. It was the most bizarre thing. Weirdly, my mum had only told me a few days earlier that it had belonged to her parents. I looked up the meaning and there were lots of dark ideas about what it signified, so I took matters into my own hands. I decided that the broken knife meant there was something I needed to let go of in my life, and I was soon shifting the focus of my work. Perhaps it was my grandparents guiding me towards a simplified career path.

Now, over to you . . .

- What superstitions were you raised with, if any?
- What superstitions do you find yourself noting or using now?
- And I'd like to set you a challenge. A simple one. I'd like you to look out for white feathers and, every time you see one, make a wish.
- Also, as you see slugs and ladybirds, black cats, numbers such as 13, or 111 – which is thought to be a spiritual set of numbers – what meaning can you derive from them?
- How does it feel, to associate these things with something positive happening?
- Are you able to shift any negative or fear-mongering superstitions to positive ones?

Remember that you can also ask for signs. If you're feeling unsure about something or someone you can say, out loud, "Give me a sign," and see what happens.

Intuition

Over the last few years, "intuition" has become a buzzword in business. A recent *Time* magazine article revealed that top executives "leverage feelings and experience when handling crises. Even the US Navy has invested millions of dollars into helping sailors and marines refine their sixth sense, precisely because intuition can supersede intellect in high-stakes situations like the battlefield."[36] But, for some, questions such as: "What's your intuition telling you?" or "What would happen if you went with your gut?" or "Just listen to your heart," can cause an element of panic. *I don't know what my intuition is telling me*, you might think.

In brief: intuition is your inner knowing; that gut reaction you have when something feels really wrong or really right. It is the ability to understand something instinctively, without the need for conscious reasoning. And if you follow it, powerful things can happen. I recommend fully engaging with your intuition to design both your home and working life (easier if you're self-employed, but in these times of flexible working, there are sometimes options for alternative ways of working when you're employed, too). Following the "rules" will make you a carbon copy of all other business owners, but following your "gut" unleashes innovative ideas and creative solutions.

When Steve Jobs was 19, he spent time in India, searching for some kind of enlightenment. Years later, he reflected on what made his trip so profound and he said that returning to America was, for him, more of a culture shock than going to India. "The people in the Indian countryside don't use their intellect like we do," he said. "They use their intuition instead, and their intuition

---

[36] "The U.S. Military Believes People Have a Sixth Sense", Annie Jacobsen, time.com, 3 April 2017

is far more developed than in the rest of the world. Intuition is a very powerful thing, more powerful than intellect, in my opinion. That's had a big impact on my work."[37]

He said that, after seven months spent in Indian villages, he saw the "craziness" of the western world, as well as its capacity for rational thought. "If you just sit and observe, you will see how restful your mind is. If you try to calm it, it only makes it worse, but over time it does calm, and when it does, there's room to hear more subtle things – that's when your intuition starts to blossom and you start to see things more clearly and be in the present more. Your mind just slows down, and you see a tremendous expanse in the moment. You see so much more than you could see before. It's a discipline; you have to practise it."

While, in the western world, we may tend to veer towards the rational, we do also use our intuition every single day. You get up and you decide what the first thing is that you are going to do. Do you go to the bathroom, chat to your partner or scroll on your phone? You decide what you want to do in that moment, led by your intuition. You then decide, at some stage, what to eat for breakfast. Again, you are listening to your body and mind and needs and following them towards a breakfast that feels intuitively right. Sometimes you'll get it wrong: perhaps you'll eat a bowl of muesli because that's what someone else in your family is having and it's on the table. It might not be what you want, but it feels convenient. Rather than follow your intuition and do what feels intuitively right or exciting, you are doing what feels easiest. But if it's not what you want, you won't enjoy it so much. And that's why, when you have that instantaneous moment of "knowing" – that gut feeling – it's best to go with it.

Moving on from the morning routine and taking intuition into the workplace, it might be that you receive an email from

[37] *Steve Jobs*, Walter Isaacson (Little, Brown, 2011)

a potential new client asking to work with you. But perhaps there's something about the email that makes you feel uneasy. You might not be able to put your finger on what exactly: maybe they're asking for too many details and it feels a bit dishonest, or perhaps you feel the writer doesn't understand you and your work properly. Or you might have a feeling that they are going to rush you through a project that needs a longer timeframe.

> Whatever it is, you have that instant intuitive reaction to the email that makes you question whether you want to work with the client.

Often, the instant reaction you have is absolutely linked to how you will be treated if you go ahead and work with that client. Intuition is strong, based on the myriad experiences we have throughout life, and our understanding of the people we work with. For instance, if it is a client situation that feels intuitively wrong, that's probably based on your experience of other clients you've worked with. And so the further into your career – and life – you go, the more in tune you will become with your intuition. That awkward feeling you have when someone strikes up a conversation and you can tell they will just take from you without giving (perhaps you start to feel tired or drained)? That's your intuition telling you this is not a match.

Outside work, too, you might find yourself with an instant "knowing" about what you want and need. Let's say you're invited out for a drink with a group of people. This might feel like a really exciting invitation, or it might feel far from what you fancy doing. If it's the latter, perhaps it's your body telling you that you need rest – and no alcohol – or that you're seeking calm and peace rather than the potential chaos of a loud, busy bar. But if it feels like a great idea, that's probably because you need to be surrounded by people and buzz and chat, in which case, you'll probably really enjoy yourself.

However, there will be times when you just don't know what to do, both at work and for social engagements. For menstruating people, this might be cyclical (when I'm pre-menstrual, I need to stay close to home, rest lots and go easy; when I'm ovulating, I like to be in among the bustle). But it might also be that you're going through an indecisive period, or feeling anxious, in which case it can feel as if there's a mist lying over your intuition.

If that's where you're at, and you feel like you're not sure how to activate your intuition – or just don't know what you want or need, or who to trust – here are three simple exercises you can do to remind yourself that you have the power to reconnect with your intuition.

Scented candles

Go into a shop that sells scented candles. Pick up various candles and have a good old sniff. Which are you most drawn to? There will probably be one that just feels like the right fit. And that's because your intuition is guiding you to it. Perhaps you'll be more drawn to lavender, known to be calming, if you're feeling on edge. Or a zingy citrus scent might catch your attention if you need a little lift. Maybe it will be an earthy aroma that draws you in, if you feel you need to be more grounded or connected to the earth. Whatever candle feels right to you, in that moment, is indeed the correct choice. Your body, mind and spirit are guiding you to it. Trust yourself and go with it.

Herbal teas

If you have herbal teas at home, open the drawer or cupboard and pull out a selection. Open each box and take a good sniff of the teabags. On the box, it might say what that tea is good for (calming, relaxing, immune-boosting and so on). But don't read the box for now; follow your nose. Only once you've decided on the tea you'd like to drink, check the box for what this tea is meant to help with. See if it aligns with what it is that you need right now.

Take a walk

Go on an unplanned solo walk, with no fixed destination. Step out of the door and choose whether to go left, right, or straight ahead. Walk. Look up at the sky. Look at the road or path ahead. Look around you. Where are you being drawn to? Why? Follow your feet, your heart, your intuition. Walk for as long as feels good. Breathe in the air. See what ideas land in your mind. Turn back whenever you fancy it. There are no rules; be guided by your inner knowing.

Intuitive posting on social media

I had a message from one of my coaching clients recently. She asked: "How do you decide what to post on social media, and when?" She said that she enjoyed my posts and wanted to share stories in the same way that I do, but she wasn't sure how to find the ideas, what to write or when to post them. She said that, sometimes, she'd have an idea, but then as she started writing it, she'd wonder whether it was interesting and lose the motivation to post.

I think this is a common experience. It can feel exposing to share our thoughts and ideas on social media. We never know exactly who's reading them and there might be a fear that we're being judged unfavourably. I have been on Instagram, writing about my work, since 2015. So as I write I am eight years in and I've lost my inhibitions. I've also found my flow. And I'm completely guided by intuition.

So I told my client that I never schedule social media content in advance, as it just doesn't work for me. It feels robotic and boring. Also, when I've used scheduling apps in the past, I tend to forget there's a post going out, so I'm not there on Instagram, or whichever social media platform, to respond when people engage. So, now, I will have an idea drop – usually off the back of a conversation, a book I'm reading or something I witness happening – and I'll start to construct it into a social media post in my head. I like to share a story that also serves as a lesson of some sort, or that has a moral at the end. I write each post quite quickly, edit for errors, adjust any awkward words or phrases, then share it.

The further into your work you are, the easier this becomes. You start to see what makes people respond to you on social media and instinctively feel drawn to create more content such as that. For instance, I have written about being a working mother in social media posts as well as in articles. One morning, I was walking home after dropping my kids off at school, thinking about all that

I am and do and want to be. I pulled out my phone and started dictating my thoughts into it. Once I'd finished, I scanned back through, changed a few words, screenshotted this piece of writing – it was like a prose poem – and shared it on Instagram. It said:

"I want to have kids and to be with the kids all the time and I want to be alone so that I can write and I want silence and peace and noise and chaos and I want to stop and rest and to keep moving and having adventures and I want to have more kids and to never be pregnant again and I want my family to grow and my family to stay the same size and I want to grow my business and to be a full-time poet and a career woman and to prioritize my children and I want to earn loads of money and I want to live on less and I want routines and an unpredictable life and I want to be calm and fierce and vulnerable and empowered and kind and firm and I want nothing and I want it all."

I put my phone away and got on with my work. When I opened Instagram an hour or so later, I had more notifications than usual. I checked the post and saw that it had been liked thousands of times. Not just that, it had been shared hundreds of times, too. Soon, people were messaging me saying: "Paloma Faith has shared your poem." "Have you seen that Busy Philipps has put your poem on her profile?" It felt quite surreal. I've had poems go viral before, but none that I'd written so quickly and shared without any real thought. That was an example of an entirely intuitive post, shared intuitively, that skyrocketed. It captured people's attention because they could relate, and because I'd shared from the heart.

- Let go of all expectation: there is no "should" with intuitive posting. Post what you want, when you want.
- Remember that posts with soul capture people's attention. A moving story, something surprising or shocking, a new and exciting insight.

- Get really clear on who you are and who your audience are. Make note of the types of posts they respond well to. Keep that in mind.
- Don't sit at your desk, desperately searching for content ideas. Go out. Walk, talk, look, watch, listen. Empty your mind; fill your mind. And just see what lands.
- If nothing appears, talk to a friend. Tell them you're feeling stuck. Ask them how they'd describe your work, in a line. See if it sparks any ideas.
- Take it to your community. Tell them you'd love to help them and wonder if there's anything they'd like to know . . .
- When you have your idea ready and feel excited to start the conversation, remember: nothing is perfect. And hit "publish".
- If you are a "doer" you will move forward . . . imperfectly. If you allow fear to stop you, you remain stagnant. Be a "doer".
- Once you've shared a post and people have started responding, note how it feels in your body. Log that sensation of sharing something that resonates.
- Over time, see if ideas drop more quickly or naturally. I expect they will.
- When they do, and you keep sharing them, your process will speed up.
- The more you share, the more people respond and the more confident you will become.
- Now, intuitive posting will be happening without you even realizing.

Intuitive business goals

When I was 29, I'd had my first baby, lost my job as a copywriter for a film-streaming company, desperately put out feelers for freelance writing work and then started my first online platform: The Early Hour. I applied to join a free Prince's Trust business scheme and was invited on to a four-day programme, where I learned the basics of running a business. It was brilliant.

I created a business plan for The Early Hour, with projections and notes on competitors, then I presented the business plan to a board of entrepreneurs. They got to decide whether I'd go through to the next round, where I'd be given a business mentor. It was a bit like being on *Dragon's Den* or *Shark Tank*, just not televised. Thankfully, the board saw merit in my business and I was accepted on to stage two.

However, I never did make the kind of money from The Early Hour that I'd predicted. I thought cash would flow in from sponsored content and, while it was one (small) income source, it didn't bring in what I'd hoped. Instead, my platform led to me getting a deal to write my first book, *The Freelance Mum*, and with the momentum which that brought, I launched an online course. It was then that I started making the kind of money I'd hoped to from The Early Hour. In some ways, it was linked – many of my customers had been readers of the articles on The Early Hour – but it wasn't a direct link.

From that point on, I stopped creating business plans and started to be more intuitive in terms of my business decisions. I would get a sense that an online course was going to go down well with my community, get to work on it, share my excitement online in the lead-up to opening sales and – sure enough – every single course sold enough spaces to make it well worth launching.

As I noticed how many of the women I was connected with on social media were saying they felt a lack of confidence about starting a business – selling, promoting themselves, sharing content on social media – I came up with the idea for my second book, *Shy*. When this book was published – reframing shyness as an attribute, not a flaw – I started to attract more shy and introverted coaching clients. I was delighted.

Now, every step I take forward, backward or to the side is intuitive. I no longer worry about what people will think if, say, I go from offering straight business advice to injecting a dose of SQ. I know, intuitively, that it's right to be sharing whatever it is I feel inspired by and that this then draws the right people towards me.

If you work for yourself – freelancing, or running a business – part of your job might entail pricing up products or services. It can feel like a fine art, but it's also an intuitive one. We will be led by what others selling something similar are charging, what we want or need to earn and how we value what it is that we're selling.

You can ask yourself these questions, when working out what to charge:

- What would you like to charge for your product or service?
- What amount feels exciting?
- What are your business peers charging for something similar?
- Where would you like to sit in the market?
- Close your eyes, put your hand on your heart and ask yourself: what is the right price for this?

Go with whatever comes up. See what happens. And then decide where to go next.

When you run a business – or work for an employer – from a place of inspiration and excitement, that will shine through. However, if you're running a business from a place of desperation, panic and simply doing what you think you should be doing, that leaks out too. And it isn't very attractive.

So listen to your body, your mind and your heart. If a strategy is generally thought to be really effective but feels rubbish to you, don't do it. There are always other options. Think outside the box. Share the things that inspire you, make you feel alive and give you energy. And you'll inspire others, make them feel alive and give them energy. Then they'll likely buy your products or services when you tell them about those in a way that feels aligned.

New business ritual

When I moved to Somerset, I was invited to a party. There, I met a woman called Rebecca who would go on to become a treasured friend. At this stage in my life, I have a good sense of who I will connect with and friendships tend to deepen quickly. This happened with Rebecca. So when she invited me to her birthday well-wishing ceremony, I was excited. I knew it would be magical. It was being led by a woman called Isla Macleod, a local ceremonialist, activist and healer and the author of *Rituals for Life: A guide to creating meaningful rituals inspired by nature.*

A few days after the invite, I was spending a night away with my middle child. We were wandering around the shops and I saw a book about rituals in the centre of the window display of a lovely, independent bookshop. I thought it would be good for my research. As I pulled a copy from the book shelf, I noticed the author was Isla Macleod. The same woman leading Rebecca's birthday ceremony in the woods.

This felt like a lovely alignment. Not a coincidence, I don't believe. This was meant to happen.

That night, back at our hotel, my son watched fireworks out the window and I opened Isla's book. The first page I opened was about creating a ritual for your new business. I was in the process of writing this book and thinking about how I might grow a community around it. The timing felt perfect.

Isla writes that, when naming a new business, "It is important to consider the identity you wish to create and how the name looks and sounds. When you have landed on the perfect name, crafting a ritual to celebrate its birth is a wonderful way to support the business flourishing in the world."

She recommends printing a poster with the business name, or creating a vision board with the name at the centre and surrounding it with images that reflect your hopes and dreams for the business. "You can also imagine your business as an animated entity and draw or find an image or sculpture that reflects its personality or essence," she says. You can then take it out into nature and find a beautiful spot in an open sacred space. Isla suggests setting an intention for the business and thinking about the inspiration behind the name. She says you could say the name aloud, in a rhythmic way: "To ripple those vibrations out into the world." Isla suggests that an additional way of rooting your new business into this world is to plant a tree with your colleagues, or anyone working with you on the business, as a way of honouring your shared commitment to this new venture.

In the business world, things often feel rushed and lacking in intention, so this is such a beautiful way to create ceremony and ritual around the naming and launching of your business.

MY SQ JOURNEY

Laura Alvarado, forest school leader, eco-therapist and founder of Meadow Education.

I was brought up Catholic, from both my mum's and dad's sides. I felt like I was touched by the sacredness in the candles and incense at church. I was an altar girl, too. I definitely felt that reverent feeling in church. But also, when my parents took me and my sisters away on holidays. We always wanted to be by a swimming pool, but they would take us to ruins and Neolithic monuments. Seeing those gave me a similar feeling to that of being in church: I recognized that some places felt very sacred.

Around the age of 13, my mum started taking me to yoga with her and there would be meditation at the end. That was actually in a church, on a mezzanine level. It brought me into a more eastern world of spirituality. But also my mum and dad always had loads of friends of different faiths – Zoroastrian, Hindu – so we went to lots of weddings involving different spiritual beliefs and religions. If I ever lost something, we'd all say a prayer to St Anthony. Spirituality was in our everyday lives, not just on a Sunday.

I loved looking through my mum's things as a child. She always had essential oils, and she had her astrological chart in a folder. Mum and Dad would talk about things that were unexplained by science. They would sometimes have synchronized dreams. And, growing up, my dad had dreams that were premonitions, so I was always aware of something out there that is greater than we can understand in our everyday lives. That always made me feel curious.

I'm listening to an audiobook called Wintering *at the moment, by Katherine May, who had a breakdown aged 17. Her breakdown sounded depressive, but I had a breakdown that was more about anxiety. I started working with Dr Bach Flower remedies and, when I was 18, went and trained with a homeopathic remedy maker. That was the first time I was discovering something myself, without my parents introducing me to it.*

I like to approach spirituality almost in a childlike way, being playful with it and not taking it – or myself – too seriously. Being reverent and respectful of spiritual traditions, but without being too pious.

SQ and my career

During the pandemic, I closed my premises – which had been an indoor space – and I realized I hadn't been content working with children in an indoor space. Since childhood, I've always been happier outdoors. I loved collecting little stones, arranging them, making potions and mud pies. It's common for children to play in that way, but I feel it connects to something primal within us, where we have that relationship; plants are our allies.

Gradually, I've listened to my higher power and, by listening, it's led me to doing this work. When I listen and try to connect with my soul nature, I receive little whispers and nudges and all of them have pointed me in this direction. I woke up one day and suddenly thought: I want to train as a Forest School leader. It was a bit of a lightning bolt moment. And the same happened with eco-therapy training: there was a sudden decisiveness. It made so much sense and it all fell into place. But I think there had been a longing, or an urge, before that.

Also, it's important to learn to listen carefully to your own dissatisfaction and not just accept that you have to grin and bear your lot. It's wonderful to know you can change your life and create a new direction in a way that makes you feel more alive.

SQ and nature

In eco-therapy, there are two levels. Level one is us going out into nature and having experiences. Level two is coming to the profound realization that we are nature. Embodying the feeling that nature is part of you and you're part of it; there's no separation. People can experience this when looking at the stars, or at other awe-inspiring moments, or also in a gentle space such as the side of a river, or even in your garden.

When we live indoors and so much of our lives are spent in manmade spaces, rather than spaces that have natural organic forms – we often live with lots of right angles and flat space, for instance, or without natural materials – we can forget that we are a part of the Earth. So, when we come back to it, it feels so right.

I like to learn about how our eyes "read" information with fractals. For those who are sighted, when we look around us in natural spaces, it's not jarring; it's like we're coming home. But it's also about finding what our natural terrain is, the one we feel most akin to. Some people like dry heat and desert space. Some people need to be near the ocean, or a jungle space, or woodland. When I travelled as an adult to El Salvador, where my dad is from, I felt at home. I have an Australian friend who lived all his life in Australia; he's in his sixties now and he's a psychotherapist, before that he was a general practitioner doctor. He travelled to Ireland, where his ancestors were from, and he cried, feeling, "This land is where I'm from." And, leaving it, he felt some grief. Our natural terrain as individuals is not always necessarily where our families are from, but we can feel really connected in certain natural spaces.

My SQ routine

As a mother, I find it hard to keep up a routine, so it can fluctuate. I try to take the outside in, so, if I'm not able to go outside, physically, into a natural space, I can connect with it through meditation and breathing.

I start the day with quiet time, indoors or out. And I have a prayer that I read (it says "God", but it can be whatever your idea of God is):

"God, direct my thinking today so it be divorced of self-pity, dishonesty, self-will, self-seeking and fear.

"God, inspire my thinking, intuition and decisions. Help me to relax and take it easy. Free me from doubt and indecision. guide me through this day and show me my next step.

"God, give me what I need to take care of any problems. I ask all these things so I may be of maximum service to you and my fellow man. In the name of the steps, I pray. Amen."

It's a 12-step prayer. I start the day remembering that I'm not in charge; I can do my best to be in control of what I can be, but I'm not in charge. This opens me up to not thinking I'm God, basically. And to being able to hear the messages from the Universe. Because sometimes we are in a period of our lives where we're so busy, and things are so intense, that we forget to listen. There's an idea that if you're too busy to meditate for five minutes, you need to meditate for ten: I feel I need to remember that. I can be a very "go", very "do" person. So, at the start of the day, I pause for a moment and remember to be in a curious place of wondering what this day will bring.

I try to spend some time in nature every day. Even if it's just walking around the streets near me, in London, I'm looking out for all the signs of change in nature. So, at the moment it's winter and I'm noticing the leaf buds in the trees that will bloom in spring. I feel as though they are buds of hope. Then I see rowan berries. In a time of climate crisis, that means noticing that autumn is really late this year. Noticing the differences. If you start doing that over a number of years, you can see them more clearly.

At night, Jesse – my son – and I each say:

- *Three things we're grateful for.*
- *Two things we're proud of from that day.*
- *One thing we could have done differently.*

It's about keeping the events of that day in the day, with humility and gratitude. And, to me, it's important to do this with him. I feel I'm being humble with him, as a parent. I msight have messed up that day and have a regret – I might wish I hadn't shouted, for instance, or had done something differently – and I hope that I'm instilling in both of us an idea of self-awareness, self-reflection and handing the day over. It's done now. The most important thing is awareness, and learning from it.

My SQ toolkit

I collect treasures, but they're not always in my pocket.

*I connect with things for a period of time. I was finding that my son was pushing my boundaries for a while, so I had a **silver necklace with a bear** on it that I'd wear. I felt connecting with the bear spirit helped me to feel really earthy, strong, solid, unmovable.*

*At the moment, I have a **beeswax candle**. When I need to tap into the spiritual space within myself, I light that candle.*

*When I have a **herbal tea**, I really feel like I connect with that plant. At the moment, I'm working with a herbalist and I'm connecting with hawthorn.*

*Sometimes, if I've done something I'm scared of and I'm in nature – so I'm scared of heights and if I've climbed up high – I try to find a **small stone** that I can hold and it embeds my bravery into it.*

*I try to use **herbs** that I can dry and grow rather than those flown over from another country; which means they are* over-harvested, which makes them a rare plant. I try to use things that are around me, in my land.

SQ books I'd recommend

The Magical Year: Seasonal celebrations to honour nature's ever-turning wheel *by Danu Forest*

A practical book, but one which also shares myths. It's based on a Druid calendar, so it takes you through the Celtic wheel of the year and connects you with different festivities such as the winter or summer solstice, or the spring or autumn equinox. I like connecting to where we are, in the seasons, and this book gives you meditations, prayers and crafts to do during each.

The Book of Symbols: Reflections on archetypal images *(Taschen)*

I like to turn to this book if I've had an interesting dream. It isn't a dream dictionary, but if I've dreamed of a train, let's say, I open to that page and the book will talk about trains in a historical way. It might reference trains in paintings or films. And it will talk about the psychological symbolism of trains. It helps me to be with that message, or symbolism.

Inner Work: Using dreams and active imagination for personal growth *by Robert A Johnson*

This is about using dreams and active imagination for personal growth. I like to tap into the unconscious, bringing those unconscious messages into consciousness. Again, this is connected with dream work, but it can also be connected with making art.

The Intuitive Body: Discovering the wisdom of conscious embodiment and akido *by Wendy Palmer*

A book I can open and read just one paragraph. I've had this book for years and it's very good for my body, to connect my body with my spirit. I've found it really helpful, as I'm very sensitive to other people's energies. The author talks about leaning back, leaning forward and finding where your centre is.

SQ in the world
Scientists on SQ

Many scientists are atuned to the elements of SQ that help them in
their more scientific understanding of the world.

"My religion consists of a humble admiration of the illimitable
superior spirit who reveals himself in the slight details we are able
to perceive with our frail and feeble mind."

Albert Einstein

"There are only two ways to live your life. One is as though nothing is
a miracle. The other is as though everything is."

Albert Einstein (again)

"At the outset of this work I most humbly and fervently pray to God
the Father, God the Son, and God the Holy Ghost, that remembering
the sorrows of mankind and the pilgrimage of this our life wherein we
wear out days few and evil, they will vouchsafe through my hands to
endow the human family with new mercies. This likewise I humbly
pray, that things human may not interfere with things divine, and that
from the opening of the ways of sense and the increase of natural light
there may arise in our minds no incredulity or darkness with regard
to the divine mysteries."

Francis Bacon, 1st Viscount St Alban

"God is known by nature in his works, and by doctrine in his revealed
word."

Galileo Galilei

6

TAROT AND ORACLE
CARDS

When I was finishing my time at school, I started applying for university. I wasn't sure I actually wanted to go, but it was what everyone else around me was doing, so I started looking into different courses. At first, I thought I'd like to be a performer, so I applied to study music, drama, dance and performing arts at various universities. I did some auditions and was offered a few places. But then I panicked. *Perhaps I want to be a writer*, I thought. So I started the application process again, while working as a waitress to raise money so that I could go travelling. I applied to study creative writing and was offered a place on a course I liked. It sounded fun: writing poetry, stories and – eventually – a novel.

I saved some money, went off travelling around Thailand and India, and when I returned, I had a fun summer of hanging out at arts festivals, including working at the prestigious Edinburgh Festival. Come September, I was packing my bags to move to the University of Liverpool, into student halls . . . and I wasn't really feeling it. I had a boyfriend in London who I didn't want to leave and I still wasn't sure I even wanted to go to university. I liked working and earning money. But I went along with it, got my student loan, made some friends, got drunk, went on an amazing writing weekend with my tutor and the other students on my course, wrote some poems and had a bit of fun.

However, a couple of months in, I returned to London for a visit. While sitting with my mum, I realized I didn't want to return to university. And, though I suspect she was probably disappointed, she didn't show it. Instead, she said: "Why don't we get the oracle cards out and they might help you to work out what you want to do?" I liked this idea. So she opened up her box of fairy oracle cards and handed me the deck. I shuffled it, while asking the question: "Do I want to return to Liverpool?" I then fanned out the deck so I could pull out three cards. I laid them in front of me, understanding that the card on the left would represent the recent past, the middle card was connected to the present and the right-hand card was about the future.

I can't remember which cards I pulled, but I know that they told me not to return. What was happening, during that reading, was that those cards were an SQ tool that enabled me to access my subconscious mind. Really, I knew I didn't want to go back to Liverpool, but it can be hard to get clarity on our true desires when there is so much conditioning around what we're "meant" to do. In this instance, I was worried about looking as if I'd failed, dropped out, not persevered, chosen a relationship over study, disappointed my parents, not done what my peers were doing. But actually, my heart wasn't in it.

That day, it was decided that I'd leave. My dad drove me up to Liverpool, we collected my belongings, got a refund on the tuition fees and that was the end of that. I actually remember a family friend saying: "It's really brave of you to leave university, well done." That surprised me. All the narratives I'd had swimming around my mind were those that came with notes of failure, but this was different. For the first time, really, I'd followed my intuition and made a decision that – while it went against the status quo – answered my needs and put them above those of the societal expectations heaped on me.

A few months later, I'd moved to Brighton, where I shared my sister's bed, got a job as a waitress (again) and eventually, surrounded by people my age who were studying, decided to apply to go to the University of Sussex. This time, I was clear that I wanted to go, that I wanted to study English – as it was broader than creative writing and would potentially lead to more work opportunities – and I was ready. I didn't quite have the grades, but I talked my way in and saw it through to graduation.

> Those oracle cards empowered me to make a big decision about my life and I'll always be grateful to my mum for giving me the opportunity to use them in that way. I've since used them to make other decisions, big and small, life and work, and they are definitely one of the most powerful tools in my SQ toolkit.

Towards the end of my degree, I'd been living with my boyfriend for a year and things in the relationship weren't going so well. There were strong feelings, but I wasn't sure we had a future; it felt like he was drifting away from me. I went to see a clairvoyant down by the seafront, working out of the back of a gift shop in a small, cosy room. I loved this woman. She was older and wiser and had such warm, kind energy. I felt I could trust her. So I told her I was feeling unsure about the relationship and she laid out her angel oracle cards for me. As she turned them over, we discussed their meaning. It became clear that the relationship needed to end.

I went home to speak with my boyfriend about the conclusion I'd reached and he was angry. He said he was going to go down to the pier and burn down the clairvoyant's hut (the hut wasn't actually on the pier, but I was interested in this image). He blamed her for the end of the relationship . . . but it wasn't her who ended it, it was me, having been empowered by an outside source. I called on the wise old woman to guide me, she called on the angels to guide her and – again – the final call was down to me. She created space for me to hear my heart and soul and intuition and to be led by that.

Oracle cards

The term "oracle" is from the Ancient Greek and refers to a female priest who would give people wise – but often mysterious – advice from a god. But we don't have much information about where oracle cards were invented. One source says they were invented by a Madame Lenormand in 19th-century France.[38] But whatever the origin of the cards, the general understanding is that they are used as a tool to deliver a message from the Universe, angels, God or Source, depending on the type of oracle cards they are.

Unlike tarot cards – which have universal meaning and structure – oracle cards can come in decks of varying sizes and the cards in one deck may relay different messages than those in a different deck. Also, oracle cards can have quite a broad meaning and act perhaps more like an umbrella view, whereas tarot cards tend to go a bit deeper and be more specific. (For more on tarot cards, see page 198.)

I have a deck of fairy oracle cards, bought for me by my mum when I was a teenager. There are 44 cards in the deck with a small booklet (on page 203, there's a list of all my oracle and tarot cards, in case you'd like to look for the same). Each card has an illustration and a short phrase, such as:

- Problem solved.
- Stand your ground.
- Look inside yourself.

So you pull out one card, or three – depending on how deep you want to go with the question you're asking – and there is a simple message on the card. And you can then refer to the deck's

[38] "Tarot and Oracle Cards: What's the Difference?", happypiranha.com, 23 February 2020

accompanying booklet, which goes into more detail about what each card means.

As an example of how it works, I'll ask a question now, as I am writing, to my oracle cards. Now, this question can be really specific ("Should I leave university?" or "Will I get promoted?") or more general ("What do I need?" or "How can I feel happier?").

I'm going to ask a question that relates to my life today, which is: "Will I become a ghostwriter?" (I'm in talks about doing this.) I shuffle my fairy oracle cards, asking my question over and over again, then pull a card from the deck. The card says: "Follow your dreams." When I consult the book about this card's meaning, the first thing it says is: "Meditate on your heart's desire. Rearrange your schedule so that you're spending time in ways that are truly meaningful to you."

It goes on to say: "Sometimes it's difficult to know what you truly desire. You have so many outside influences, as well as personal fears, tugging at you, demanding: 'Pay attention to me.' You wait for a free moment that you could devote to your dreams, goals and aspirations. Yet that moment never seems to arrive. The fairies ask you to take charge of your schedule. First, they ask you to meditate on your heart's desires. Make a list of five priorities in your life. Then, write down a schedule – in ink – so that you'll spend the necessary time engaged in these activities. It's not important what you specifically do during these times; what's most important is that you invest time and energy in that which makes you happy and fulfilled. Affirmation: 'I deserve the best. I take charge of my schedule and my life'."

Now, you could read the above description and derive one meaning from it – perhaps that the card is saying I shouldn't be a ghostwriter – while I could derive another meaning: the absolute opposite. It's open to interpretation, because you use the cards to answer your own questions and you will actually already have the answer to your questions buried deep down inside. The cards simply bring what you already know, in your subconscious mind, to the fore.

I always love it when I pull a card for a client. I'll invite them to ask a question and, if we're face-to-face, they'll shuffle the deck and pull their own card, but if we're on a remote video call, I'll pull one for them. Either way, I read the description out to them. They always sit quietly, listening to the meaning, and I think: *I wonder what they're getting from this?* Without fail, they feel moved by the message. They relate it to their question and life and derive a strong sense of what they now need to do.

Generally, I find oracle cards to be a little lighter and clearer than tarot. I actually use tarot more regularly, perhaps because I like to work a bit harder and dig a bit deeper, but if you are new to these decks, oracle cards could be a good place to start.

Tarot

Tarot cards are believed to have originated in northern Italy during the late 14th or early 15th century, created for the Duke of Milan's family, but the cards were not regarded as mystical until the late 18th century, when the occult became popularized. It was at this stage that people began believing that these cards could foretell your future, as well as help you to answer questions about your past.

A traditional tarot deck contains 78 cards: 22 Major Arcana and 56 Minor Arcana. The Major Arcana represents life and its primary stages that everyone experiences, while the Minor Arcana represents the people, events and feelings that every person encounters in their life.[39]

Now, this feels like a good day for me to write about tarot and oracle cards and how I use them for decision-making, because I have found myself in a slightly confused situation that I need some help with.

In 2015, I launched my first digital platform, The Early Hour. I published articles daily and growing this platform – and its associated online following – helped me to secure my first book deal, which in turn led to me creating my online course business. I have a lot of love for The Early Hour, because it's where my proper self-employment began. Also, there are some great articles and interviews on there and it still gets about 10,000 views a month, without me ever promoting it. So it sits there, idly.

I then launched The Robora to host my online business courses and coaching programmes. I have several thousand women in that community, who come to me for business coaching, courses and consultancy.

---

[39] *The Original Rider Waite Tarot Deck*, A E Waite and Pamela Colman Smith Rider, 1999

And then, to coincide with this book, I started thinking about a platform called Raise your SQ. I was wondering if I could continue to run all three platforms. I couldn't work out how to link them up so that they all felt connected, rather than disparate.

My husband said: "Perhaps you shouldn't run all three; maybe you should just focus on one: Raise your SQ." I hear him: simplifying is always good. But I wasn't sure I could let go of The Early Hour, while The Robora was still running as a successful business. So I decided to ask the tarot cards for some clarity. I got my *Starchild* tarot cards out, shuffled them, asking in my head: "Should I run all three platforms?" I kept asking this question over and over, so I was very clear in my head about what I was focusing on and what I wanted an answer to.

I then laid out the cards and pulled one from the pack that I felt drawn to. The card was the Three of Wands. I liked that it was "three", this felt relevant. The illustration on the card had a woman sitting naked on a large rock, maybe on the moon, with three white branches stretching out from her and into what looks like the Earth. It was as if all three branches were part of her. In terms of looking for "signs", it felt wonderfully auspicious. I pulled out the tarot booklet, to check the deeper meaning.

It said: "The message: The Three of Wands marks a time in your life when you can look to the future with total clarity. This wisdom comes from having the foresight to walk your own path with confidence as you move forward. Your hard work has paid off, but it is not time to rest just yet. You are now gaining momentum in achieving your dreams and are aware of how your creativity has the potential to expand your goals to the next level. You have a wonderful system of support from friends and family members, which strengthens your enthusiasm. The Three of Wands also indicates a state of understanding. You know what it takes to reach your goals. Additional meanings: Being visionary, expanding your horizons, listening to your intuition, looking upward."

As I was reading this, I had memories drop into my mind, including a conversation I had with a family friend who was interested in my motherhood poetry. He had said it felt like I'd grown a community of women who want to connect and discuss modern motherhood. I wondered if perhaps I could connect with that community of mothers, who might be interested in learning more about my poetry, without running The Early Hour. I could do it on Instagram perhaps? I have a new book of motherhood poems (about being a working mum) already written. Perhaps I should send it to my agent, to see if there's scope for a publishing deal?

I also considered The Robora and how that has been my bringing-in-money business. But I wondered whether through this book, my work might automatically shift to being more about SQ and less about general business. I could introduce ideas about SQ over on The Robora, while keeping Raise your SQ focused on spirituality, nature, creativity, healing and magic. As I thought more about that card, the three online platforms became more clearly linked in my head as I saw myself as the naked woman on the rock: I am at the centre of those three platforms, they have come out of me. I am a mother, an entrepreneur and now I'm teaching about SQ. These have all been parts of me and my story but it doesn't necessarily mean I need to continue with all three, if in fact streamlining it would work better. With this conclusion, I felt the pressure lift.

So that's an example of how I do a tarot reading for myself, a really simple one just with a single card, when I have a pressing question that I feel needs to be answered. But importantly, I take the meaning I need that day, to free my mind of panic and indecision. It doesn't mean I make impulsive decisions, or take big risks, and I'm always open to the evolution of a situation; the path is rarely linear. So, down the line, I may find another solution to the conundrum of where to focus my energies. But the reading on that day made me feel comforted.

A tarot reading for you, right here and now

As with oracle cards, you can pull out three tarot cards from a deck: again, the three cards you feel most drawn to. You then lay them in front of you. The card on the left represents the recent past, the card in the middle represents the present and the card on the right represents the future. As you turn over the cards, asking your question, you can relate them to what's happened – in terms of your question, or the subject you are asking about – in the past, where you're at now, and where you can expect to be headed.

Now it's about *your interpretation* of the cards. No one can get deep into your mind, but you can be safe in the knowledge that you do, in fact, have all the answers regarding your own life within yourself. This is why coaching can be so helpful, as a coach will ask questions and share prompts to help you access your own answers, they won't tell you what you need to do. (If they do, find another coach.)

The tarot cards act like a prompt, pulling up the answer that you already have inside. Some people refer to this experience as accessing your higher self – either within, as in your subconscious mind, or your soul – or you might imagine there is another "you" hovering somewhere above you. They are still you, but they have some extra wisdom that perhaps the "grounded you" doesn't have. Some people also believe that there is a higher being – like a god or some kind of deity – informing the cards that you choose and the answer that they present. It's up to you to decide which makes the most sense, or feels most right.

Now, as an experiment, I thought it might be interesting if you decided to come up with a work-related question. Have a good think about what feels most pressing for you at the moment. It could be something like: how do I make more money? Or do

I want a new career? Or how do I adjust my work-life balance so that I have more time at home? Or anything else that feels important to you right now. I'm going to pull a card now and you can see how the card might help you to answer your question.

The card I pulled is the Eight of Cups. And the description is:

"The Eight of Cups represents a soul-searching journey of growth and transformation. Know that letting go is sometimes necessary for change. This could mean facing or healing painful memories, past relationships, or personal issues that are still exerting pressure on you. This release may foster an emotional strength to help you navigate how to use your own energy, or when you have to deal with the stress or baggage of others. After purging the unnecessary burdens in your life, you may find that you will seek a more spiritual path. A time for transition and spiritual awakening. Additional meanings: moving on, abandonment, sacrifice, growth, equanimity."

How does that fit with you?

Does it answer your question at all?

Remember, if it feels too broad or too specific and you're just not sure it's working for you, it might take some practice to start understanding the language used in these cards and to relate it to your own life. Keep giving it a try, though, as it's such a useful SQ tool.

Finding the right tarot and oracle card decks for you

Choosing your oracle and/or tarot cards can be a really fun, intuitive exercise. Ideally, I'd recommend finding a shop that you can actually visit in person (I've listed some on page 268). You can then hold the card boxes, look at the illustrations and – if there's a display box open – read some of the meanings. You will find that certain design styles, as well as the way that the text is written, will appeal to you more than others.

If you can't visit a shop, you can buy cards online. Some of the shops I've listed from page 268 have great websites too, or you can take a look online, using the list below, at the decks I have – and like – and see if any work for you . . .

My oracle and tarot cards
Healing with the Fairies oracle cards by Doreen Virtue PhD
These say:

"Fairies are nature's powerful guardian angels, and they can miraculously assist you with your self-esteem, relationships, health, and career. With the help of these 44 oracle cards, you can have a deeply personal relationship with the amazing fairy realm. The fairies will help you find new inner strength and confidence and guide you in treating yourself with greater love and respect. With the help of the enclosed guidebook, you'll learn how to give yourself and your loved ones accurate and helpful readings. There are no negative or frightening cards or images in this deck."

The Starchild Tarot written and designed by Danielle Noel
These say:

"An intuitive tool that connects your innermost realms and Higher Self. This 79-card deck explores the ancient traditions of the Tarot through a multidimensional journey of consciousness and awakening."

The Starseed Oracle by Rebecca Campbell and Danielle Noel
These say:

"Have you always had a longing for home without really knowing what that meant? If so, you could be a Starseed

Soul. This activating oracle will help you to unlock your soul gifts, connect with your cosmic origins and remember who you truly are."

Ethereal Visions by Matt Hughes

These say:

"In creating Ethereal Visions Tarot, Matt Hughes has drawn inspiration from the Art Nouveau movement, adopting its distinctive style and meticulous approach to craftsmanship. The artist has also created two additional cards to supplement the traditional Major Arcana. Every detailed image in the 80-card deck is hand-drawn and coloured. Each card is illuminated with gold foil stamping, to elegant effect. Incudes a 48-page booklet."

MY SQ JOURNEY
Tallie Maughan, founder of Turning Earth ceramics studios.

I didn't have a particularly religious or spiritual upbringing. My mother's family were communists and had sent her to Socialist Sunday school, so she hadn't had much exposure to religion in her childhood either. She was ethical rather than spiritual and brought us up with environmentalism as the dominant social idea. She was very intellectual and didn't have a use for superstition or intuitive tools. I thought astrology was an odd fancy of uneducated people and that tarot was something done by gypsies in old films. We used to go to the church in the village where I was brought up, because my mother believed in its role as a community hub and because it was the only place in the village except the pub where people gathered. She would point out that the vicar was wearing clothes from another century and question the rituals as a kind of human nonsense. I think that her honesty freed me to develop an authentic relationship with spirituality, and – unlike some people brought up with a religious structure that didn't seem real to them – I find churches very moving these days. Watching the Eucharist brings me to tears.

My stepfather was a lot more spiritually minded, although not vocal about it, so I didn't understand this about him until I got to know him better as an adult. He is naturally very intuitive and I'm sure that rubbed off on me in subtle ways. He was brought up in the city, but has the direct connection with nature and its wisdom that I associate with true country people. I think his spiritual openness is impacted by the years he's spent working with trees for his job. He'll say, for example, "You've got to listen to the Rosicrucians," and follow that with, "But it's not beyond them to laugh at you." I think that beautifully articulates a principle I try to live by, which is to take spirituality lightly, be receptive to intuitive messages and only loosely attached to outcomes.

While I wasn't raised with any overt spiritual influences, I had a profound spiritual experience and I think that is probably what made me not lose track of it, in the way some people do. My dad died very gracefully when I was four years old, and when my mother asked him to go to the light, he told her there was nothing but light. Just take a moment to contemplate where he must have been when he said that. Those words have had a profound influence on me throughout my life, although it took me years to be able to put myself in his place and fully understand their enormity. I don't think there's any greater gift to anyone than to understand from the person they trust most in the world that death could be that way.

His death also left me with an ongoing relationship with a dead person to work out for the next few decades, which is a little like being psychic, as you are continually relating to someone without a physical body. It's only easy to love someone who is dead in this way if you aren't too bound to the material world. The purification of death is also awe-inspiring. After someone has died and only the love remains, you understand just how powerful the love we share really is.

How I found spirituality

My first experiences of spiritual awakening came, as for a lot of people growing up in my generation in London, from going to raves and taking psychoactive drugs. I had a boyfriend who experimented a lot with mushrooms and so on, and one day in my early twenties, I took some DMT with him. DMT is meant to be the chemical that is released when the spirit enters a foetus's body when it is conceived, and which is also released into the bloodstream at the point of death. It was a profound and terrible *experience, like visiting hell. I was looking for a god and couldn't find one. I came back to Earth with the awareness that I was living my whole life the wrong way. It was a helpful realization.*

Of course, I spent several more years following the wrong path, looking for shortcuts, searching for what I thought would make me happy based on my programming, trying to work hard to buy myself the future vision I so badly wanted to achieve. However, the seeds of the understanding of the futility of my frightened egotistical approach to my life had been planted. I think this happens to a lot of people: we have an insight several years before we are mature enough to let go of an unhealthy or life-limiting pattern.

I was lucky, in my early life, to be miserable enough to desperately need help, as well as to be in quite a few hippy circles. This meant I came across a lot of teachers and received energy healing from several quite powerful, otherworldly people. I also explored the world of tantra in my twenties, and took Vipassana meditation. The usual kinds of pursuits for young hippy types.

What spirituality means to me

I'm not really a fan of the term "spirituality", as I think it has become something of an identity these days, and that it can imply there are differences between people. In fact, I find it a little uncomfortable how outwardly unconventional I actually am, how often I reference astrology for example, because I think its irrationality is quite alienating to a lot of people, as it was to my family when I was a child. "Spirituality", then, is a word I'd normally use only with some caution and contextualizing.

I think, these days, I understand spirituality as being awake to the deeper reality of things, what I describe as: "Being in the engine room of the dream," where I can see that my experiences of disconnection and misery are reflections of being in a negative dream state. I suppose to be spiritual means to be awake, to be conscious of the ways in which I am creating reality and the ways in which I am responding to it. When I connect with love and with the higher mind, things shift and flow more easily.

These days, I am committed to keep waking up from the negative dream, from my entrenched programming – what some people would call karma – and to act with agency in the world to help make it more beautiful in the small ways I can. In some ways, the actions associated with this make me less of what I used to think of as spiritual – unconditional and communistic – these days I understand that being business-like and boundaried is just as much a spiritual path, as it allows me to serve other people much more effectively.

My SQ practices

I am not particularly disciplined about practice at the moment, probably because I have two small children and not a lot of time for myself. Children are their own practice. They mirror low states of consciousness in uncomfortable ways, and when we are truly connected we see our angelic nature in them, too. The simple act of singing them to sleep at night has a quality of joy to it that keeps me in a flow state.

I practiced a lot of different things in the past, including Vipassana meditation, OSHO dynamic meditation® and yoga. I also did a lot of deeper work, which has given me what I can only describe as a direct psychic connection to enlightened personal guides. I try to check in with these as often as I can, that's really the most important action I can regularly take. I find this most powerful to do in dialogue, so unless I am in a circle with other like-minded people, it usually depends on me having a willing listener in my husband. I find that if I channel the wisdom of my guides, using the process I was taught by one of my teachers, I get reconnected with love and then things kind of slot together.

I think it's the quality of our consciousness that most helps. You can do all kinds of things from a low state of consciousness, even yoga and meditation, and not feel much better. I think the key is to raise one's awareness to a higher level and then it doesn't especially matter what you do on a practical level, the dream just kind of works.

How spirituality has helped me to succeed

I would say at this point that everything I have ever done that has worked has come from the direct guidance of a power greater than myself. This power talks to me through the GPS of my excitement and through my visions, and sometimes through the direct channel of my connection with internal guides. I see and feel traces of the future at times in a way I really can't explain. It's easiest just to follow these through the world, like a thread through a maze, and then – hey – you find yourself in a better place all-round.

My SQ Toolkit?

*I have a **pendulum**: a stone with a hole in it that I collected from a beach when I was a kid and kept in a box of treasures. My mum brought it to me at work once, and it rolled itself under my desk. I feel it speaking to me through my wrist when I use it. It's very sure and trustworthy and never feels it has to agree with me; the truest kind of friend.*

*I put **gemstones** around my house and workplaces as directed when working with people who use them, but I never really connect very deeply with those; that's not a process that speaks to my intuition at the moment. (Similarly, I have long struggles with tarot, whose meanings I think I process primarily with my intellect, which is a slow and frustrating way to do things.)*

*I learn a little more about western **astrology** with each person whose chart I look at and recently I find my intuition opens up* *when I look at a person through the prism of their Chinese zodiac year. It's been helpful for me to understand myself as a water dog. For example, it helps me see my weak points more clearly – water dogs can be disorganized and a bit heavy at times – and also to understand why fate has made so much of my life focused on the work I do. (As the saying goes, I certainly work like a dog.) Using astrology gives me a view into my blind spots and therefore the opportunity to work with them.*

*I understand the value of taking a **regular inventory** of my flaws, in order to keep growing, whether that is doing The Work of Byron Katie, or doing 12-step work through one of the fellowships. I have spent time in Sex and Love Addicts Anonymous, Co-Dependents Anonymous and Workaholics Anonymous, and they all help to bring the unconscious madness into the light of awareness.*

SQ books I'd recommend

Existential Kink: Unmask your shadow and embrace your power *by Carolyn Elliott PhD*

A book that should be more widely known. I had two coaching sessions with the author, using the principles she outlined in that book, and they changed my life. Basically, it teaches that misery is enjoyable and that the best way to have any choice about when it appears is to find the parts of ourselves that are in love with suffering and give them free rein, to embrace them with love and reintegrate them. She explains very well the Buddhist practice of Tonglen, which is about asking for the suffering of the world with an open heart. It's a way to step into power and stop resisting, to stop identifying oneself as a victim, and in doing so to find one's source and connection to love. I used these practices to reorient my relationship with pain, which naturally meant I was then more comfortable to bring joy into my life, and the much-longed-for baby appeared soon after. So much of not having what we want is really to do with being scared that we wouldn't survive losing it again. To welcome pain is to be free.

Loving What Is: Four questions that can change your life *by Byron Katie*

A classic. I still use her enquiry process whenever I notice that I've become a victim of my thoughts. I've noticed just how many miracles arise from doing that in every area of life. I am happy to realize I'm unlikely to ever be finished with Katie's Work.

The Continuum Concept: In search of happiness lost *by Jean Liedloff*

There are a lot of self-help books, but this is the book that influences me most and it's well worth reading. The book came from the author's time living with a particularly joyful tribe called the Yequena in Venezuela, and studying their childhood experiences to see why they ended up so happy as adults. She pinned it down to fulfilling the need infants have to be treated in a way that is continuous with our biological evolution. I think everything I do in life is directed at helping to restore our connection with the continuum, whether that is sleeping with my babies so they feel held safely in the world of childhood magic, or creating the conditions for thousands of people to happily express themselves through clay. Clay is a medium as ancient as we are, which I believe is strangely necessary to our hands. I think using our hands to mould clay in an evolutionarily continuous way probably helps build helpful pathways in the brain; personally I connect my use of it with the period of my life when my creative agency blossomed.

SQ in the world
Footballers on SQ

Footballers have talked about the influence of SQ
in their relationship to their sport.

Glenn Hoddle played in midfield for Tottenham Hotspur between
1975 and 1987. During this time, he had a number of injuries that
were "cured" by the healer Eileen Drewery. He'd originally met
Drewery as he was dating her daughter and Hoddle was sceptical
about her claim that she could heal his leg. But he became desperate
when it wasn't healing itself, so he let Drewery lay her hands on the
injured leg and he was amazed that he was able to play that Saturday's
match. For many years, he'd return to Drewery for healing. He never
asked her how it worked, or said anything about his beliefs (or lack
thereof), but he was open-minded enough to receive healing that
might have contributed to his long football career.[40]

David Babunski, the former Barcelona star, believes that an intelligent
mind is an inquisitive mind: "Always curious, always open to new
possibilities, always seeking new fields of knowledge. Questioning,
never blindly accepting." He believes that a human being's potential,
"extends infinitely beyond our wildest imagination."[41] On the
concept of God, he says: "The image of God as an authoritarian
entity judging from the sky . . . is one of the greatest human
conditionings and many people today are still prisoners of it. But if by
saying 'God' you are referring more to energy, to an intelligent cosmic

---

[40] *Why Me? My life as a Healer,* Eileen Drewery (Headline, 1999)
[41] "The world's most intelligent footballer? Ex-Barca star Babunski
      predicts a spiritual revolution", Carlo Garganese, goal.com,
      17 June 2017

design, to a universal consciousness we are an inseparable part of, then we have a totally different and open field for discussion."

Marcus Rashford MBE plays for Manchester United and the England national team. He's also an activist, campaigning against child food poverty and lobbying the UK government to provide free school meals for all children who need them. He has spoken openly about his devoutly Christian mother, Mel, and said, "The faith we have in God is shown by the people that we are". Selina Stone is a former community organizer who now lectures in political theology at St Mellitus college in London. She says that although Rashford and his England teammates Bukayo Saka and Raheem Sterling may not necessarily attend church, the faith they were raised with still contributes to their core values: "In some Christian practice there is a sense that faith is about assenting to a set of beliefs – you read the liturgy, recite the creeds, assent to doctrine. Black Christian traditions are more about the embodiment of faith, how you live out what you say in a Sunday service, how you are attentive to the felt needs of people around you as part of your faith commitment."[42]

[42] "God-given talent: Saka, Rashford and Sterling blaze a trail for black British Christians", Julian Coman, theguardian.com, 17 July 2021

7

MANTRAS, AFFIRMATIONS, MAGIC SPELLS AND PRAYER

When I was about 12, my friend's dad became very ill and was taken to hospital. We were close, as families, and everyone was worried. My younger brother and I prayed; it seemed like the only thing we could do. But we weren't praying to a specific god, it was more as though we were calling to the Universe to somehow help this man to pull through. (He did.)

And then when my own baby was extremely ill and in intensive care, just before the pandemic, I found myself praying again. My auntie's church collectively prayed for him too, as well as a family friend's church. Again, these are some rather lovely elements of organized religion: the coming together of a community to care for an ill child.

In times of need and worry, words can be comforting. Both the words we hear from others and the words we might recite in our heads, in the hope that they'll have the power to fix the outcome. We might find ourselves coming up with mantras or affirmations that we repeat throughout the day while visiting someone who is very ill (such as, "He's going to be okay, he is healthy; he is well"). We might also use positive statements to prepare ourselves for a work event that we feel nervous about, such as a presentation, or public speaking.

During the pandemic, when my daughter and her friends

were feeling anxious, I bought them all magic spell books. They contained rituals and spells to help with all sorts of things, such as connecting with family members, feeling more confident or making your wishes come true. We sat together with my daughter, in the garden, lit a candle and created an altar with dried lavender and she recited the spells that she felt she needed at that time. It makes me feel a little sad to think back to that time and how profoundly the pandemic affected young people, but I feel there was a small amount of solace found in the ceremonies we created together.

Mantras

Traditionally, a mantra is a sacred utterance – a syllable, word or verse – that is considered to possess mystical or spiritual efficacy. These mantras might be spoken aloud, or repeated in your mind; they can be uttered just once, or said over and over again. While the sound itself might not be linked to a word we understand, the mantra is thought to have "a profound underlying significance . . . in effect distillations of spiritual wisdom."[43] So when a mantra is repeated continuously, we can fall into a trance-like state, which takes us to a higher level of consciousness. When I was travelling around India, I often encountered the Hindu mantra "om". And in meditation practice, this sound might become elongated as it's said aloud: ooommmmmmm. (Now, mantras have taken on an evolved meaning, alongside the traditional one, which is that they are "a statement or slogan that is often repeated.")[44]

In terms of etymology, the Sanskrit word *mantra* is derived from the root *man*, "to think". And scholars consider the use of mantras to have begun earlier than 1000 BCE. In India, the first mantra was *om*, which was hummed in a meditation. The Chinese translation is *zhenyan*, meaning "true words" and the Japanese reading is *shingon*, which means "true speech". So we know that mantras are connected to words and speech and some kind of truth. And the way we tend to use mantras now, outside of organized religion, is still in a meditative way: honing in on how we *want* to feel. Here's a simple example:

My daughter was learning to ride a bike. I had a toddler and a new baby to look after and so I hadn't done a good job of teaching her, because I didn't have the energy. Therefore, she was teaching herself. I watched her pick up that bike and attempt to

---

[43] "Mantra", britannica.com, 20 July 1998

[44] "Mantra", oxfordlearnersdictionaries.com

ride it to the back of our (not very long) garden again and again. She would turn the bike around, come towards me, turn the bike back, go to the back of the garden. But what struck me was the fact that she created a mantra. Every time she picked up the bike she would say: "I can do this."

It goes back to positive psychology. If we tell ourselves that *we can do it*, we feel more able to. If she had been saying out loud: "I feel scared, I don't think I can do this," it's possible she would have wobbled and come off the bike. But as it was, she continued to do it, telling herself that she could, until she succeeded. She completely taught herself to ride a bike.

While writing this book, I decided to set myself a challenge and to see if having a mantra could help me to achieve it. It was during a breathwork/movement session – at home, alone – and I found my body wanting to go into a headstand. I'd never done a headstand, or attempted one, before. But suddenly, I had this urge to try. I decided to do it against a sofa, so I got into position and tried to lift my legs up into the air. It was extremely hard and, any time I managed to raise my legs, they'd flop clumsily over my head on to the sofa in a weird backbend. I thought: *This isn't for me; I'm not a strong, headstand-y yoga-type person.* And then I decided that was ridiculous; everyone starts somewhere.

The next day, I wanted to try again. This time, I was in my bedroom. I went into a near-headstand and then my legs flipped over my head and I landed flat on my back. Fortunately, I didn't injure myself, but it was close. I wondered if I should give up; if I might be at risk of breaking my back. But I decided that, if I was careful, it would be okay. I went over to my bed and filmed myself, so that I could make sure my elbows were directly under my shoulders for the right alignment. My friend, Lizzie, had advised me to tiptoe my toes towards my body and fold my legs in towards my bottom before lifting them straight. And I started saying: "I can do this, I can do this, I can do this."

You know what? I did it. I did a proper headstand. And I got it all on camera. From flipping and flopping all over the place to legs up straight, in the air, and holding it for some moments. It was amazing to note the shift I felt as I said those positive words again and again; it helped me to focus and get clear on my goal. *It worked.*

Research has shown that concentrating on positive words can change the shape of your brain. Over time, given sustained positive thoughts, functions in the parietal lobe (the part of the brain that processes spatial sense) start to change. Consequently, this changes our perception of the self and those around us.[45] Herein lies the power of the mantra: positive words, repeated, *literally change your brain* and you feel differently about yourself and those around you. Absolutely wild and wonderful.

So how can you use mantras in your life? And how is this related to SQ?

Well, much like my daughter did with learning to ride a bike, every time you tell yourself that you *can* do something (go for the job interview, make the pitch, whatever it may be), you make yourself more likely to actually be able to. I wrote earlier about how you can start your day by deciding to focus on positive thoughts and words, so saying: "Today is going to be a good day," could be considered a useful mantra for, in fact, having a good day.

And in terms of this becoming a spiritual experience, you might like to close your eyes, sit cross-legged on the floor as you would in yoga or meditation practice, and imagine you are surrounded by a beautiful light, or a sense that you are somehow being protected. As you imagine this, and say your mantra out loud, you might like to believe that this energy around you is there to make sure that your mantra comes true.

---

[45] "The Neuroscience Behind Our Words", Lindsey Horton, brm.institute, 8 August 2019

Affirmations

Affirmations are closely linked to mantras. They are declarations either about who you are, or who you want to be. Here's an example that I am always a bit embarrassed to share . . . but here we go. When I was in my twenties, I was living in London with some friends and I was single. I wanted a boyfriend and so, every morning, when I ran around the park behind my house, I would say to myself, on repeat: "I am beautiful, confident and successful." I would say these words in time with my feet hitting the floor, literally repeating them the whole way round the park. I really hammered into my head that this was a truth (even if, at first, I didn't particularly feel it) and, in time, I must've exuded some kind of beauty, confidence and success, because I met the boyfriend who would go on to become my husband.

It's important to say the words of an affirmation in the present tense, as if it is already happening. So, if there is something work-related that you want to happen, make sure that you are creating an affirmation that puts your success in the present tense. For instance:

- I am so good at job interviews.
- I am earning £100,000 a year.
- I am improving people's lives, through my work.

Even if these things haven't happened yet, you want to really sink into a meditation and say the affirmations in the present tense, so you start to trick your brain into believing they are happening right now. Or, to put it in spiritual terms, you want to "embody" the experience. Close your eyes, breathe into it, imagine the affirmation has happened and is happening now.

- How would you feel if it was happening now?
- How would it feel in your body?
- How would you feel around other people, if you had this success?

Feel into it, breathe into it, imagine that it is absolutely happening now and repeat your affirmation again and again and again.

Now, we've talked about mantras and affirmations, which are both about creating positive statements to say out loud or in your head, to yourself. It's time to get on to the more out-there side of things.

Magic spells

First, a story.

When I was in my late teens, I moved to Brighton, on England's south coast. I'd walk around the maze of old streets called The Lanes, popping into all the spiritual and "witchy" shops there. I loved them. In one, I picked up a black magic spell book. At the time, I had a boyfriend and I wanted him to be utterly in love with me. He may have been already, I'm not sure as I think I had pretty low confidence back then.

Anyway, I flipped through to a spell about love. I had to focus on the lit flame of a candle and imagine my boyfriend just above it, walking towards me as if I was a magnet and he was being pulled in. Then I had to say the words of the spell out loud, which was all about him being drawn to me. I would repeat this magic spell over and over again, every night. I was truly committed to making him fall in love with me. I think he did, eventually.

And then one day, he turned to me and said: "You've put a spell on me." I didn't know if he was joking or not, I was a bit panicked. But the truth is, I had. It showed me that perhaps there is something in these magic spells. I don't know whether it is actual magic, or the fact that again – by focusing on what it was that I wanted – I had put myself in a better place to make it happen. By believing that he would be in love with me, I manifested that reality.

Now, I use magic spells in business. There is a nice short spell that goes as follows:

"Zeus, Zeus, king of gods, pour down upon me the generosity for which thou art justly famous."

When saying this, I look up to the sky and imagine a big, strong, male, god-like figure floating up there who is transferring some crazy energy down to me. His arms are spread out at either side and it seems as though he is emanating something – like lightning – that is striking me. Except that it's a very positive thing. It's powerful. I say those words over and over again, continuing to imagine Zeus pouring this energy down on to me.

In the middle of the pandemic, when my family of five was living entirely off the income we were bringing in from my online course and coaching business, The Robora, I would stand in the shower, washing my hair and body and almost aggressively recite the spell, demanding that Zeus pour his generosity upon me. I liked the masculine energy of it and that I could make this demand. I felt empowered and like I was taking control (with Zeus's help, of course).

Another spell I like, to counter the masculine Zeus spell, is a more feminine spell recited to the goddess Vesta:

"Oh wonderful and generous Vesta, goddess of home, hearth and harmony, bring me money and prosperity this day, shine your radiant face on my finances today, bring me all the money I need this day. Thank you, oh divine mother goddess, for thine glorious and generous help."

For this one, I imagine a beautiful female goddess, also up in the sky, and as I look up towards her, again her arms are outstretched and she is glowing with a golden light. Her long wavy hair is floating out all around her and, as she looks down on me, she is smiling. She has this lovely energy and she is transferring it from herself on to me, via golden rays.

When I first started saying this, the Vesta I was addressing with my magic spell had round cheeks and quite a glowing white face. In time, interestingly, her face has become my own face. Now, I am looking up at a version of myself, in the clouds, and praying to her. She could be my Higher Self.

I also have a prayer or spell, that feels slightly more religious, though when reciting it, I'm doing so from a place of spirituality rather than Christianity. It goes:

"Bountiful Lord, creator and sustainer of the Universe,

thou who hast made the heavens and earth so overflowing with abundance, flood my life this moment with thine goodness. Let all good things be mine, this day and every day."

For this one, I close my eyes and really imagine the energy of the Earth emanating up into my body. It's a good spell to do while standing on the actual earth – on soil, or in water – while imagining that you are absorbing all the energy of the Earth around you. I close my eyes, say the words, feel as if I am connected to the Earth and the Earth is connected to me; we are one and the same. And I can really feel as if I am soaking in this powerful energy.

Lastly, I use a magic spell that goes:

"I am powerful, I am strong, I am invincible and forever masterful. All good things come to me because I am strong, powerful and commanding. I attract power, riches and all things that are beautiful."

With this one, I really do imagine that I am powerful and strong in my body and mind. And the whole way through, this is the focus, until right at the end, when I always imagine beautiful parts of nature in my mind and how I'm attracting lovely plants and outdoor experiences into my life.

I use these spells, or incantations, when I'm launching a new course, or pitching an article or book idea. It helps me to feel as though I am somehow supported by something bigger than myself. So I'll get clear on the course I'm launching and who I want to attract and I might set myself a goal, either financial (such as to earn £10,000) or numbers (to get 100 sign-ups). Setting a clear goal and then using a combination of magic spells with a visualization – transferring the glowing energy of your heart to the hearts of all the lovely clients you'd like to attract – massively elevates a launch. It makes it more fun, energized and magical. And that's what running your own business should be. It can feel daunting running a business on your own, so feeling that someone else has your back – even if, really, it's just you having your own back – can feel like a relief.

Once I've opened sales in the lead-up to a launch, or when I'm preparing to send off a journalism pitch or book proposal, I will be saying all four of the above spells daily, often twice a day. Sometimes more. I will look up to the sky as I say them, or down to the Earth. I will close my eyes and really feel into the words I'm saying. It can be embarrassing if someone walks in when I'm doing it, but it really helps me to get clear on what I want and to believe that it will happen. I might go for a walk in nature and say the words on repeat. Or when I'm lying in the bath. As I feel into the words of these magic spells, it's like my body and mind are being charged up. Suddenly, it's not just me doing the work, but there is something else at play: a god, energy, spirit, Source, Universe . . . something outside of me is lifting me up and propelling me forward.

You might like to look for your own spell book, or use the spells that I have mentioned above. I've memorized them so that I can say them wherever I am and whenever I want. This means, if I'm going on holiday, I can secretly take my magic spells with me. I've also created some new magic spells, just for you.

Five magic spells for success

The best way to perform magic spells is by candlelight. This way, you can use the flame as a focal point that will bring you into the present. As you gaze into the candle flame, say the words below – out loud – and allow your body to be filled with the belief that a higher power will deliver what it is that you are requesting.

- Money
  "Show me the path to riches and abundance. Light the way. Take me by the hand and lead me there. I am ready to receive."

- **New clients**
  "Bring me the ideal clients, every time. Bring me the clients I dream of working with. Bring me clients whose values match mine and with whom I can do wonderful work."
- **Creativity**
  "Shower me with creative ideas. Allow my mind to open up and capture them. Remind me that I am creative, capable and full of bright and brilliant ideas."
- **Closing a deal**
  "This deal is going to happen, and it's going to happen now. Be there, with me, as I close the deal and move forward with this project."
- **Something exciting**
  "I am ready to receive exciting news. Exciting news about something unexpected that will bring me joy, happiness and gratitude. Thank you."

Prayer

When I was travelling around India, aged 18, I wandered into a beach bar in Goa. There was a hippie-looking man in there with a notebook and pen, leaning back on some cushions. I asked what he was writing and he read these words aloud: "God, grant me the serenity to accept the things I cannot change, the courage to change the things I can, and the wisdom to know the difference."

I said: "Wow, that's powerful, did you write that?" He nodded at me: yes. But he was lying. It is called "The Serenity Prayer" and it's used in Alcoholics Anonymous. Fibs aside, though, these words are pretty powerful. In life, there will be things we can't change, things we can and the need for us to understand the difference. Remember, if you choose to recite this poem, you don't need to envisage God as a grey-haired man in the sky. "God" can be an energy surrounding you, a Shamanic cloak, a beautiful woman – or child – sitting next to you. You get to decide.

MY SQ JOURNEY

*Caroline Till, designer, researcher, co-founder of design agency
Franklin Till and curator of the critically acclaimed "Our Time
on Earth" exhibition at Barbican.*

*I wouldn't say I grew up in a spiritual home, but there was an
openness to ideas that were perhaps more on the periphery.
For example, my dad left when I was quite young, so we went
through healing as a family. I remember the tools my mum turned
to were considered "alternative". She had reiki, she would talk
about an osteopath instead of a chiropractor. So that all seemed
normal to me. My mum engaging in those practices would have
influenced me. I've always been, as a researcher by profession,
interested in things at the periphery.*

*We weren't religious, but we would go to the abbey where
we lived every Christmas and the choir there was incredible.
My mum wasn't teaching us about religion, rather, our visits to
the abbey were about the experience of something greater than
yourself. She would expose us to experiences that felt ethereal.
Even now, I'm obsessed with choral music. But Christmas was
always about the spiritual element, for us, rather than religion.*

In Alain de Botton's book The Architecture of Happiness, *he
describes a church and the way it's specifically designed to make
you believe in something you don't know to be real. I find that
fascinating: how spatial environment, or the fabric around you,
can influence your mindset. He describes huge vaulted ceilings
and all these other design cues that are intended to make you get
on board with religion. It's so interesting.*

SQ and the planet

*Working in sustainability, what drives me as a designer
is always the role of design in responding to the climate*

emergency, a situation that we have created as humans. I'm a massive optimist, in terms of the climate emergency, and I believe that design has the power not to solve all the problems necessarily, but to shift mindsets. And we've never needed to shift mindsets more urgently than in the current predicament. So I've been on this journey for the past couple of years, to redefine my definition of our relationship to the natural world and to ourselves.

In terms of spirituality, there are two things that have recently happened which make me more inclined to engage more deeply with what you might call spirituality and spiritual practice.

First, there is a very current dialogue in the environmental space about the need to connect with yourself before you can connect to others and to the planet. To look after and nurture yourself. I've developed a deep relationship with The Bio-Leadership Project, which is all about supporting people in leadership roles to work more in tune with nature, but also, to look after themselves. They've given me tools, such as breathwork (see page 25). I did a nine-month fellowship with them, online, through the pandemic. Every session felt a bit like a hug. We'd start with breathwork, so you can connect with yourself and remember you're not a machine, you're a living being. What they taught me, that I took into the exhibition at Barbican – "Our Time on Earth" – is the meta narrative that we're living beings in a living planet, and isn't that amazing? That felt so resonant because the climate emergency, particularly in design, can often be doom-mongering. It felt like the right narrative to me: not chastizing me or making me feel shame, but making the climate's future feel like an open opportunity.

I went on one of the Project's wild camping retreats, about placing yourself in nature. They run these "solos" when you spend 24–48 hours alone, in nature, camping. They're there, but only in the very far background. The impact it has is that you *become able to see the micro stuff that is happening in nature. By having no stimulus and just time – but, simultaneously, no real sense of time – you feel at one with, or "of", nature. I said to the leaders at the end: "This is the first time I've felt looked after." As a mother and running a business with 11 team members, I feel a mothering responsibility. So it's really nice to feel mothered myself.*

Second, with the Barbican exhibition, we started with a narrative that we are living beings in a living planet. We in the west can have a perception that suddenly we're all about connecting to nature, that it is somehow a fashionable modern thing. We needed to say that this isn't new, it is deeply entrenched in many cultural philosophies from indigenous people from all over the world. We have an obsession with looking to the west for what's new . . . and we needed to subvert that.

We worked deeply with a group of indigenous leaders from Brazil. We wanted to give them a platform to showcase their world philosophy. To show that, for so many years, they've had this deep connection to the natural world. They don't see themselves as separate from it. I think that's the biggest problem in the west: we have cultivated a view in which we are separate from nature, that somehow we are above it and we rule it. So we engaged with these amazing women – Célia Xakriabá and Sônia Guajajara – who are at the front line of protecting the Brazilian rainforest.

We commissioned a film from them and they said they wanted to write a letter to nature called "We Are Earth". So they wrote that love letter. But Barbican's parameters included that we needed to keep in mind our visitors' dwell time and attention span; they didn't want any film longer than two minutes. The "We Are Earth" film lasted seven minutes. We had a meeting, Barbican said they had to cut it, so they went off again. But, when they came back, it was still seven minutes long. In that second meeting, they said to us: "Well, we spoke to the spirits and the spirits told us it needs to be seven minutes long." For me, that was brilliant. We had other conversations in which they said of themselves, "We speak in the language of dreams," while referring to us in the west, colloquially, as, "People of merchandise." I thought: yeah, you're right.

SQ and connection

I picture our clients sometimes, sitting in their corporate offices, and I think we all need to remember that we are part of something far bigger than ourselves. "Interconnection" is the word I always come back to. That's what we were trying to do in the Barbican exhibition: to show that everything in the biosphere is deeply interconnected. People are working in such siloed ways, we need to bring back the interconnection.

So now we bring in breathwork (see page 25) at the beginning of meetings, especially with some of the bigger corporate clients. It changes the whole dynamic. At first, people think it is weird. I guess it's out of their comfort zone. But then, it changes the tone of the meeting. Suddenly, people are connected to each other and to themselves.

Through working with these amazing people in the Barbican exhibition and The Bio-Leadership Project, I feel a sense of responsibility. How can I bring these tools into the work that we're doing with other people, to help shift these conversations? We don't have the time, now, for incremental change – due to the level of impact we've made as humans – so I wonder how we can get there more quickly. That might sound counter-intuitive, as many of these tools are about slowing down, but they're also about getting to the crux of the conversation.

How do we take these tools to clients and change both the way we're working with them and the nature of our collaborations? And how do we use them to nurture our own teams?

We're now a remote company, so it feels more important than ever to explore how we connect with each other. I am going to ask a breathwork practitioner whether she'd facilitate a session each month for our team. I really feel there's a new paradigm of being a remote company. There are amazing benefits, such as the flexibility: one team member lives in a van in Portugal with her partner and their dog. But, on the other hand, we always jump straight into meetings, without the peripheral conversations you'd have in an office. Our productivity has gone through the roof, which is amazing, but then how do we make sure that people are okay?

My biggest ambition for next year, in terms of how we look after the team, is to cement the in-person days and make them not about work, but about something else. We had a really beautiful session last year during which we made wax flowers. So how do we give our team tools to look after their wellbeing and be connected to each other in body, mind and spirit?

SQ in nature

For me, spirituality is going out into nature. I need to remind myself that I am very small, insignificant in relation to the bigger picture. Since moving to Somerset in south west England, I can't help but see this: going for a walk with my husband every Friday has become a spiritual ritual. Once a week, we are part of something that is far bigger than ourselves. Forests do that for me.

SQ books I'd recommend

The Overstory *by Richard Powers*
This is a novel in which the author tells the story of a forest, and it's a deep story of interconnection. Really, for me, it makes you aware that you're part of something way bigger than yourself. The author writes that we need to shift all of our storytelling

to be telling stories that speak to our deep connection to the natural world. As a designer, it made me think of the power of storytelling through design.

Entangled Life: How fungi make our worlds, change our minds and shape our futures *by Merlin Sheldrake*

People talk about mycelium, fungus and fungi all the time, but I read this book to understand more about the role of mycelium and – basically – they are the foundations of everything. The nodes of interconnection of most things in the biosphere. And I found this book really beautiful. The author is fascinating, because he's a scientist but with a very spiritual approach.

SQ podcasts I'd recommend

The Long Time Academy *podcast*

The Long Time Academy *loves to help people shift to "long time thinking". They say that we've been existing in short-term thinking. A lot of their long-term thinking approaches are based on "seven-generation thinking", the idea that everything we're doing should be designed for seven generations in advance. Or "cathedral thinking", the idea that you're never going to see results in a lifetime, so your thinking and ideas are building for a future. The Academy encourages people in corporate settings to have an empty seat that represents the "child", to make them think about the future implications of their decisions. I found this series so inspiring.*

SQ in the world
Public figures and entrepreneurs on SQ

Public figures on how their SQ helps shape purpose and direction.

"What's clear is that the mental health crisis is a downstream symptom of a larger crisis: a crisis of meaning, a crisis of a world in need of spiritual renewal."

Arianna Huffington

"It isn't until you come to a spiritual understanding of who you are – not necessarily a religious feeling, but deep down, the spirit within – that you can begin to take control."

Oprah Winfrey

"Spirituality is meant to take us beyond our tribal identity into a domain of awareness that is more universal."[46]

Deepak Chopra

"Practising spirituality brings a sense of perspective, meaning and purpose."

Brené Brown

"If you lose money you lose much. If you lose friends you lose more. If you lose faith you lose all."

Eleanor Roosevelt

"I love going to temple. I love all the rituals."[47]

Padma Lakshmi

---

[46] "Exclusive: Deepak Chopra Explores the Evolution of God", Dan Schawbel, forbes.com, 25 September 2012

[47] "Beautiful and damned", Jess Cartner-Morley, theguardian.com, 8 April 2006

AN INTRODUCTION TO SHAMANISM

Rhonda McCrimmon is a Celtic seer and shaman from Scotland, focusing on creating shamanic pathways for those who have been disconnected from their animist heritage (the belief that everything possesses a spiritual essence). She has been on a shamanic path for nearly a decade and recently founded the Centre for Shamanism. Here, she shares an introduction to Shamanism and offers ways to incorporate the practices into your everyday.

Shamanism is an ancient nature-based spirituality, surviving for thousands of years in some form across every inhabited continent on earth. Shamanic practice begins with a helping spirit guide and with an animistic belief.

Our guide/s are with us whether we know them or not. All it takes is to cast a thought to our spiritual team to become aware of the support available.

Shamanic people are conscious that everything has a spirit and a soul, including manufactured objects such as your car and laptop.

Combining these basic principles creates surprisingly simple everyday shamanic practices that can support spiritual intelligence.

Developing a relationship with a guide

Shamanic guides come in many forms. Angels, animals, myths and legends, deities and ancestors are the most common examples. To meet a guide, follow the simple steps on the next page.

235

- Light a candle and sit with the light, holding the intention that you are only available to meet a guide who will support you in your life.
- Listen to some steady drumbeats or other relaxing music.
- Allow your imagination to connect with your intuition and see what comes. You might not see a guide. You may have an inner knowing of what or who your guide is. If you feel your guide is a crow or other animal, you're on the right path. You can have more than one guide.
- When you feel complete, you can thank your guide for making itself known to you.
- Extinguish your candle with gratitude, to close your space.

Now you have a guide; you can build a relationship in the following ways:

Continue to sit with your guide in a sacred space, as above, and ask questions. Ask questions about how you can improve your life now and what steps you can take to achieve your desired future. Be curious; the more you ask, the more you'll learn. A small caution is to avoid fortune telling. Focusing too much on the future rather than the now will dilute your experience and is usually wholly ineffective.

Think of your guide in the evening before you sleep and again in the morning; this only takes a few seconds and will set you up for helpful dreams and an energetically protected day.

If you're having relationship difficulties with a partner, friend or work colleague, cast your mind to your guide and invite them to surround you and protect you from unpleasant external energy.

When you are out and you find yourself feeling drained, ask your guide to surround you and support you to keep your energy within yourself and the energy of others separate. It helps to have a visualization of your guide surrounding you with light, a bubble or a cloak.

Nature connection

This is a shamanic mindfulness exercise to bring one's attention and focus back to nature. Noticing details such as whether the wind is gentle, or which direction it is blowing, brings one back to a state of rest in the body and out of fight, flight, freeze or fawn (becoming a people pleaser). Shamanic nature connection is a quick and easy way to allow your body to regulate your internal nervous system back to a place of safety. Conscious connection also allows more apparent intuitive connection and understanding in daily life. There are many things you can try:

Breathe in fresh, crisp winter air with your eyes closed and notice what emotions come up for you. Any feelings you wish to release can flow away as you breathe out.

Walk barefoot on grass and think of your ancestors walking the same way. Please give thanks for their life and for giving you life. You can connect with only the loving ancestors if you prefer not to communicate with all of your lineage for any reason.

Omen Walking is also a nature-based practice that can easily be incorporated into busy lives. This technique is helpful when you need an answer to a challenging question in your life. Go for a walk where you live (this can include a city, nature is everywhere). Think of the help you need and ask that the Universe and your guides help you to see omens, signs and synchronicities that will help you with this issue. Then walk with an open heart and allow the Universe to speak through your experience. Omen Walking can take practice, but it is a powerful shamanic tool.

An example of Omen Walking in practice might be to hold the intention that you would like a sign about whether you should look for a new job. On your walk, you might notice a few babies and a truck with the words "a new way" on the side. You may realize that babies mean something new and that a new opportunity may be the way forward for you; the words you notice back that up. You can then sit with those signs and feel your way to the best decision.

Family- and home-based practice

If you like a clean house, then a shamanic spring clean will be up your street. This technique can be used monthly as maintenance, or after a problematic relational interaction with family or friends in your space. Open a door or window and, from the opposite end of the house, use a rattle, smoke or other vibration such as your voice to chase any unwanted or harmful energy out of the open door or window. Get into corners, under beds and behind furniture as you do this, as stagnant energy can collect in the places that don't see much light or movement. Children enjoy this process, especially using rattles. Teaching our children these basic practices will help them develop healthy spiritual intelligence from a young age.

Giving offerings is an essential part of shamanic practice. It's also another engaging way to involve children. Offerings should be a small sacrifice and not something you would throw away anyway. Offerings are a form of gratitude practice. Give offerings of milk with oats and honey, or herbs you have bought or collected. You can bury these in your garden, a forest you like to walk in, or another appropriate place. Bury your offerings while saying thank you to the Earth for your food and nourishment. Giving offerings teaches our children to be grateful for our Earth and not to take her gifts for granted.

Practices for work

Bringing a shamanic connection to a working environment can enable profound shifts in energy levels and life force maintenance and help to maintain boundaries and positive relationships.

Creating a sacred space around you, whether you work from home, in an office, vehicle, school or hospital, is simple and effective. Ask your guide to set your space and that anyone who enters your space is invited to a place of peace and open dialogue. This simple ritual works in any environment. It's essential only to invite others to peace; anything more is not ethical. Trying to change others without permission is a controlling and emotionally immature action that will open you to negative external influences.

When you sit down at your computer, take a minute to give thanks and ask that the information you need is readily available. Being grateful for our work equipment, instead of other more negative thoughts, can support a shift in energy towards the enjoyment of the working space. Connecting with your work equipment, such as your laptop, can also help a more effortless flow of creativity and connection.

Shamanism is not a religion, but a set of principles that bring you back into balance with the external world and your internal landscape. Get creative and see if you can develop some daily rituals to support the growth of your spiritual intelligence.

SQ EXPERIENCE: SHAMANIC HEALING

When I moved to Somerset, I was having an online conversation with a woman called Chloe. She told me she lived in Somerset and we soon realized that I was moving to the same town. We met and Chloe told me about some of the amazing work she was doing. A few months later, Chloe told me she had trained to be a Shamanic healer. I was keen to have some healing and she agreed to me having a session. I was a bit nervous. Although I'm totally open to any new experience like this, I didn't know what would be involved.

I arrived at Chloe's house and could hear wind chimes tinkling as I walked through the door. Her front yard made me feel as though I was in India, Thailand and a beautiful part of England's coastline all at the same time. It felt like the seaside and also as though I was in a temple. We walked through to the beautiful garden and got comfortable in the studio there, sitting on cushions and sheepskin rugs. Chloe lit a candle. She opened by asking how I was and I shared some of my thoughts – and conundrums – about my work. I wanted clarity on how to simplify my business.

Throughout our hour-long session, Chloe brought in sound – channelled through her body – to help heal me. She sometimes looked as if she was pulling something up and out of her throat.

I was led on a meditation, through woodland, and invited to meet someone or something. I saw a blue jay bird up ahead. I was told it might have a gift for me and the bird, in my mind, handed me some water. As we went deeper into the meditation, I felt my arms wanting to lift at each side of my body and flap, like wings. At first, I felt embarrassed, but I decided this was a safe space to let go. So I let my arms flap and I imagined I had the power to lift my body into the air and soar through the skies. Interestingly, I often dreamed of flying, as a child. Perhaps I was being taken back to that. When I woke from the meditation, I was back in the hut with Chloe. This meditation experience, and how it actually took over my body, made me realize how powerful the mind is and where it can take you, if you let it.

Healing the home

I mentioned earlier about the haunted house I have moved to (see page 160). Well, after experiencing a handful of incidents that I didn't feel very comfortable about – lights turning on and off in the middle of the night, the feeling that I was being pushed into the wall – I asked Chloe to come and do a Shamanic cleaning of my home. She arrived with a bag of wonders: sage, candles, a drum, feathers. I went to my office to work and Chloe moved through the house, calling out to the spirits to ask what they wanted. I heard banging, singing, loud guttural sounds.

The idea with a house-cleansing like this is that you are asking old energies, or spirits, to leave so that the new residents (in this case: us) can claim the space and settle in properly. It's thought that old spirits may linger if there's something unresolved, so Chloe asked the spirits what they needed.

She said there was a man turning the lights on and off because he was angry about the garden. I know that, some years ago, the previous owners of our house built a house in the garden and fenced it off, dividing the land into two. This spirit, George, told Chloe he wanted us to plant a fruit tree and then he'd leave. I bought a pear tree, a fig tree and a blackberry bush. I planted them, happily. I love gardening and I loved the idea of answering this restless spirit's wishes.

Since Chloe came that day, I haven't experienced any weird goings-on in the house. Some friends that I've told about this episode have looked at me as if I was being ridiculous, but I've decided that doesn't matter. If a cleansing like this makes my home feel more welcoming to me, it's worth doing.

8

BRINGING SQ INTO THE WORKING WORLD

A few years ago, my best friend Lizzie was getting married and I was tasked with arranging the hen (bachelorette) party, along with two other bridesmaids. For some, a hen party might mean lots of alcohol, strippers and other (perhaps) fun – but not hugely meaningful – elements. But I knew a woman who ran beautiful women's circles involving yoga, intention-setting, a gift of some sort, chocolate and opening up, so I pitched it to the other bridesmaids and they were, fortunately, open to it. The bride-to-be was, too. But what she didn't tell me in advance was that lots of her friends, who'd be coming along, were pretty dubious.

We arrived in a lovely light room in London, with mats laid out. After a relaxing yoga class – lots of stretching and breathing – we gathered together in a circle and sat cross-legged on the floor, the bride-to-be in the centre. We were each given a piece of paper and a pen and were asked to write a memory, anecdote or thought about our friend. These memories were all gathered and put in a glass jar for her to take home. We then shared something, openly, while she sat there in the middle.

There were tears. There was laughter. It was the most magnificent way to connect us all – Lizzie's friends and family – as women, sisters and people who would be attending the wedding.

Lizzie said she loved it. And the friends who'd been a bit worried or unsure about it were really moved, too. They felt it had worked well as a way to honour Lizzie. There is something very vulnerable about gathering together, in a circle, and sharing like that. Opening your heart and baring your soul. And I think that, within the workplace, we need more of this. Rather than bitching through emails and getting fed up with the hierarchies that exist in organizations, we could adopt a new approach to how we work alongside others.

I have shared this hen party example with you because many of the people who came that day had been sceptical about doing something that felt pretty out-there. In a workplace environment, there will be SQ sceptics, but that doesn't mean they can't get on board with what I'm going to suggest next. Again, all that is required is an open, curious mind and a desire for change and compassion. When people open up, they need to trust that they are supported and feel safe.

Circle

Whether you hire someone to run your circle, or do it yourself, you might like to include some of the following:

- Cushions laid out in a circle to sit on. This way, everyone is equal, on the same level, sharing the same space.
- In the centre, you can create an altar. Lay a small tablecloth and place a candle and ornament on it.
- You can have a scent diffuser spraying a calming scent (such as lavender) around the room, or light a stick of incense and waft it around the space.
- Each person in the circle could have a piece of paper. On it, they can write an intention, fold it over and place it on the altar. They might like to share their intention, but they don't

have to. It can be work- or home-related; something they'd like to see or feel happen.

- You can use chimes or a Tibetan singing bowl to "dong" at the start of the circle to "open" it.
- Someone can guide a short meditation. I experienced a circle recently where we were asked to close our eyes, take some deep breaths and go somewhere in our minds we'd never been before. Once there, we would meet someone. They would hand us a souvenir and share a message with us. People might like to share where they went, who they met, what the souvenir was and what the message was.
- There can be a crystal, wand or candle passed around the room and, with it, each person is given a chance to speak. Questions to ask them might be: "How are you feeling at work right now? What would you like to see happen? What excites you?"

Remember, this is a confidential space. People should be able to speak freely without fear of retribution or gossip. What happens in the circle stays in the circle. If you run the company and would like to discuss anything that comes up with your employees, this should happen after the circle is closed, and only with their permission.

To close the circle, each member could close their eyes, make one wish for themselves, one for the group and one for the business. Thank everyone for joining, blow out the candle, bang the drum or gong and the circle is closed.

SQ work meetings

I went to a harvest lunch at a farm in Somerset. It's a yearly event, where people from the local village come up to the farm to enjoy food made from the land. There were about 200 people there.

Before the food was brought out, a local vicar invited us to close our eyes and say a form of grace. As we sat together, giving thanks for the food and closing with an audible "amen", I thought: *What a lovely way to open this event – connecting us all to each other and the experience.*

Saying (a form of) grace

Imagine if we opened work meetings with the same moment of gratitude? Well, we could. Whether gathered in a room face-to-face, or on a video call, instead of diving straight into how to make more money, we could assign one person to play the role of secular "vicar" to open the meetings with words along these lines:

"Thank you for being here. I invite you to close your eyes for a moment, take a deep breath in through your nose and exhale through your mouth. Let's breathe together, for three breaths. I'd like to give thanks to you, for the work that you do, and to our clients who keep us in business. Also, to our manufacturers and to everyone – here and not here – who works with us to keep us functioning."

You can go round the team and ask each person to say something that they feel grateful for that day. They could offer one thing they're grateful for related to work, and one connected to home.

Workplace mascot

You could create a workplace deity, a mascot, who is present at meetings and brings luck to the proceedings. You might like to spend time together, as a team, thinking about what this could be. It could be an animal that represents what you're trying to achieve, or an ornament that feels appropriate. If you all work remotely, you might like to all find your own mascot – based on a shared word, or theme – and bring it along to online meetings.

Think of a word, or theme, that represents the work that you do. Decide whether you'll have one team mascot, or each find a mascot – or make a clay figure – representing this. While together, close your eyes and imagine that you are transferring the energy you want from this mascot on to it.

You can create an incantation that you all recite while looking at the mascot. It could be: "Bring us luck, prosperity and abundance."

Bring your drum, chimes or gong to use at the start and end of meetings.

Remember, this doesn't all have to be done in a really serious way, it can be fun. It's about bringing you together as the team that you are and instilling a notion of togetherness, hope, joy, gratitude and forward-thinking. When we feel seen, heard and aligned with our collaborators, we create our best work. Also, as the "boss", you can create a work environment that feels so nourishing, creative and enriching that your employees see work as a tonic that feeds positively into their home life. Imagine that? Revolutionary.

SQ tips for boosting your confidence at work

Confidence is key to success, which is why we're constantly bombarded with articles in magazines such as *Forbes, Oprah Daily* and *Psychology Today* giving us tips for improving our confidence and self-esteem.[48, 49, 50] And it's no wonder there's a demand for these articles, with a massive 79 per cent of women saying they struggle with low self-esteem.[51] When we believe in ourselves, we go for that job (even if we don't match all the criteria), launch that new product or pitch for that book deal. All of the tools I've shared so far will – I hope – have helped you to believe in yourself, encouraging you that you can work towards a life that feels more fulfilling, balanced and exciting. Now, in this final chapter, I'll bring it all together by sharing ideas about how these spiritual tools can be used in specific and common work situations that might usually leave us feeling anxious. Here are some examples:

Pre-meeting nerves may be calmed by doing a *tarot reading before a work meeting*, to help you to work out what outcome you'd like. Rather than focusing on shaky hands, or panicking that you might forget what you want to say, you can focus on the cards in front of you and the message

[48] "10 Ways To Build Confidence", Frances Bridges, forbes.com, 21 July 2017
[49] "Build Your Confidence in Five Seconds – Really!", Elena Nicolaou, oprahdaily.com, 19 January 2022
[50] "5 Steps for Increasing Your Self-Esteem and Confidence", Robert Taibbi, psychologytoday.com, 7 August 2022
[51] "Majority of women struggle with self-esteem issues", Alison Simpson, wearethecity.com, 8 March 2021

you receive, then head into the meeting feeling clear on what you're contributing and where you'd like this to lead.

For those suffering with fear of failure (this affects women more than men and can impact their career development and decisions[52]), it can help to *focus on past successes*, in order to visualize future success. *Create a manifestation list*, so that you know what it is you're hoping to achieve. This might include manifesting a pay rise, new clients or a better relationship with colleagues.

For a daily reminder of your greatness and capabilities, set *positive affirmations* to pop up in the reminders on your phone. Every time one of these messages comes up, you'll receive a lovely boost. They might be messages such as: "You can do it." "Your career is in your hands." "You have great potential." "Dream big." "One step at a time."

Practice the law of attraction thoughts and beliefs. For example, if you have a difficult meeting, don't hold on to anger and resentment: instead, reframe your thoughts to be more aligned with what you would like moving forward. That might include wanting to be seen and heard, to feel empowered, to be respected. Focusing on the negative (failing, becoming invisible, being left out of future talks and so on) might mean you opt out. Focusing on what you want will help you to work towards the positives, ensuring positive outcomes.

---

[52] "Gender Differences in Fear of Failure amongst Engineering Students", Krista Nelson, Danielle N Newman and Janelle McDaniel, *International Journal of Humanities and Social Science,* vol. 3, August 2013

SQ in the world
Psychotherapists on SQ

Psychotherapists have openly discussed the importance of SQ.

"Healing comes only from that which leads the patient beyond himself and beyond his entanglements with ego."

Carl Jung

"In some ways, I was very disabled but I had this sense of otherness and spirituality. I am very practical and pragmatic, but I believe in a different kind of order. There are patterns in the world and in people's behaviour."[53]

Camila Batmanghelidjh

"In indigenous cultures around the world the natural world is regarded as the realm of spirit and the sacred; the natural is the spiritual."

Ralph Metzner

"I have learned that my total organismic sensing of a situation is more trustworthy than my intellect."

Carl Rogers

"Rituals and routines are both about delineating between space and time and creating a grounding rhythm, a predictable structure with a reassuring, calming, and stabilizing effect."[54]

Esther Perel

---

[53] "How I made it: Camila Batmanghelidjh", Ella Alexander, glamourmagazine.co.uk, 11 May 2015

[54] "Letters from Esther #19: Routines and Rituals", Esther Perel, estherperel.com

MY SQ JOURNEY

Rosamund Dean, journalist, editor and author of Reconstruction: How to rebuild your body, mind and life after a breast cancer diagnosis.

I was raised with no religion at all – my parents are both atheists. Because my family are very rational and science-based people, I was brought up to think that was the best way to be. They would eye-roll a little about anyone who had a spiritual endeavour.

I'm generally interested in health, wellbeing and ways to be happier and healthier, though. In recent years, there's been a shift towards science acknowledging practices that might have been considered a bit more out-there 20 years ago. When I was 22, in my first journalism job, none of my friends would have meditated or manifested or any of that. But now, there's so much science behind the effect these practices have on your brain – what happens if you take that time to meditate, do yoga, practice gratitude, do journaling. There are scientific studies saying these things can have a powerful effect on your brain and that they are good for energy, focus, concentration.

If you look at all the tech bros in Silicon Valley who are all mega-rich and super-successful, they're all spending their money on ways to "biohack" their bodies and there's a big focus on cognitive health. Though the tech bros would probably describe it as "cognitive optimization". Lots of them are employing amazing scientists who are saying how important it is to meditate.

When Rhonda Byrne's book The Secret *came out, all about positive thinking and the law of attraction, I thought it was nonsense. But then I read neuroscientist Dr Tara Swart's book* The Source *and thought:* this is exactly the same as The Secret, but this author has explained the science behind it. *So making a vision board focusing on what you want isn't going to make those things happen because of magic, or because the Universe is listening, but because your brain has become primed to focus on those things. Dr Tara Swart would say, because of focusing on what you want, your brain has got you there. I think you have to keep an open mind. These things that may previously have been perceived as a bit mad, have now been proven by science.*

The physician and author Gabor Maté talks about illness and the mind–body connection. People have been dismissive of this in the past, almost thinking that the theory is a way to assign blame – if you're ill it's because you didn't think in the right way – and that has put people off being open to the idea. Now, there's so much research behind lots of Maté's work on stress and trauma and the chronic illnesses that can be caused by it. I heard an interview with him recently and he said: "If I could delete one phrase from science and medicine it would be 'evidence-based'. People dismiss something if there isn't a big clinical trial proving it, but you can't always have those clinical trials. Anecdotal evidence is evidence; one person's experience is still an experience, you can't just dismiss it."

There are lots of elements of religion that I think are so important: community, gratitude, charity, singing as part of a group. There's research about how people with some kind of religious faith tend to be healthier and live longer. I think it is down to all of those elements that make up organized religion, rather than religion itself. But I can't know for sure.

What I do believe in is the subconscious mind. It was quite stressful after my cancer treatment finished, because I had to look out for signs that it might have returned, but it was hard to know what those signs might be as they can be very varied. So after yet another trip to the oncologist, who sent me for a scan because of my symptoms – though nothing showed up – I thought: maybe I'll try hypnosis to try and reframe my thoughts. I think it helped.

The hypnotherapist I worked with had a session with me and recorded it, with my permission, so I could listen back to it every evening before bed. I saw her a week later and she asked how things were going. I said: "Fine, but I don't really think I've heard the recording, as I just fall asleep." And she said: "That's good, because in the time between being awake and falling asleep, the messages will be going on but your conscious mind isn't arguing with it." I have definitely been feeling a lot more positive.

I also believe in the placebo effect. If something works for you, it works. That's unarguable. Within the cancer community, people swear by acupuncture, reiki, cold-water swimming . . . so many different things. They say, whatever their placebo is, that it's so good for their health, or relaxing, or galvanizing. But another person, for whom that experience would not be so enjoyable, wouldn't get the same benefits from it. So I do think it's very individual. If you're the type of person that is inclined to believe that a reiki session is going to be very good for your nervous system and therefore for your immunity and your general health – and I do believe it works that way – then it will have more of a positive effect than if you went into it thinking it would be a waste of time.

I went to a women's circle and it was an amazing experience, I loved it. You don't have to be super-spiritual to feel the sense of community and sharing in that environment. It's so good for people, emotionally, to do that. The leader gave out cards and we had to look at their meaning. I remember someone else had a similar card to mine, with a butterfly on it. I said: "I think this butterfly represents a sense of rebirth, because of the cancer treatment, it's almost like being in a chrysalis and I'm going to come out of it and be renewed and totally different. And maybe even better than I was before." The other person in the group with a butterfly said: "This really speaks to me because butterflies are really beautiful and colourful and the card is all about creativity and how I need to access my creativity more." We took such different things from the same card. I'm inclined to believe that things like that circle work because they make you think about what you want and need in life, and how you feel about things. The card sparks something in you. And that's a kind of magic.

SQ practices

I used to get up in the morning before my kids got up and meditate. I did that during my cancer treatment. I tend to go through phases with it. I'm better in summer when it's lighter and warmer.

I've tried journaling, but it doesn't work for me. Especially if I'm going through something hard: writing about it feels a bit depressing.

Gratitude is really important. I don't make lists, but in the conversations I have with people, I try and focus on what I'm grateful for rather than the hard things. When we're having dinner with the kids, I ask them what the best thing is that happened to them that day; I try to get them to focus on positive things.

I do yoga, though I haven't practised regularly for a while. For me, that comes in phases as well.

Over the past few years, my dreams have been around health. My hypnotherapist recommended I make a vision board with yoga images, a healthy-looking old person and so on, basically things that make you feel: I am a healthy person who's going to live for a long time. I haven't done it yet, but occasionally I see a picture on the internet and save it for my board.

SQ books I'd recommend

The Source: The secrets of the universe, the science of the brain *by Dr Tara Swart*
The Expectation Effect: How your mindset can transform your life *by David Robson*

HARNESS YOUR MENSTRUAL CYCLE TO GET AHEAD AT WORK

Raising your SQ means connecting more deeply with "spirit", but also with body and mind. And, for menstruating people, this means getting in touch with your cycle. Here, women's health expert Le'Nise Brothers explains the menstrual phases, and what you'll be best (and worst) at during each of them. Le'Nise is a yoga teacher and registered nutritionist, specializing in women's health, hormones and the menstrual cycle. She is also the host of the Period Story *podcast, which aims to break taboos around menstrual health and hormones, and author of* You Can Have a Better Period.

Picture this: you're at your desk, frantically trying to come up with some new creative ideas for a project, but you're drawing a blank. You're frustrated because only one week ago the ideas were flowing and you felt so excited about all the possibilities ahead. Now, all you want to do is finish the projects you've already started and get through your to-do list. You're scratching your head, wondering why you don't feel the same way every day.

If you've ever worked in an office, you'll know that our working days tend to have a familiar rhythm. There's an expectation that we'll bring high levels of energy across the entire day and we'll be able to work in the same way, day in and day out. But the dramatic changes in the working landscape over the last two years have challenged this thinking, with working from home forcing companies to acknowledge that a different way of working is possible.

For those of us with periods and a menstrual cycle, we're still working with this cultural expectation that we have a 24-hour rhythm and that we'll feel the same way every day. We won't. We have an energetic, physical and cognitive cycle that matches with our menstrual cycle, or the time from day one of our period until the day before our next period starts. This cycle can be anywhere from 21 to 35 days (remember: it's completely normal not to have a 28-day menstrual cycle). Within this cycle, we have a number of physical, cognitive, biological and hormone changes that guide us, rather than control us.

Once we understand these changes, we can tap into a power that gives us a competitive advantage at work, whether we have a 9am–6pm day, or work for ourselves. This power changes our expectations for ourselves, allows us to plan our working day and week differently and enables us to give ourselves a little grace when things don't go to plan, or we're simply struggling to focus.

If we think of our menstrual cycle as having four phases, analogous to the four seasons, this knowledge can help anchor the way we plan our working lives.

Let's start with the first phase, menstruation, or our inner winter.

This is a time when we'll want to go a little bit slower. Our energy is at its lowest point (but crucially, not completely depleted), alongside two of the major hormones that guide our menstrual cycle: oestrogen and progesterone. Low energy means that we'll naturally turn inward and become more introspective and intuitive. This is a time to focus on tasks and projects that require evaluation skills, such as preparing for an appraisal or *spending time working on your business, assessing what's working and what isn't and planning for the future. You might use this time of deeper insight to set new goals or intentions for the month ahead.*

*Once we finish our periods, we move on to the next phase, the follicular, or our inner **spring**.*

Similarly to April and May, this is a time when we start to feel a bit more like our true selves, coming alive with ideas and hatching plans for new adventures in our working lives. Oestrogen, our feminizing hormone, is rising and this leads to rising energy, as well as an increase in brain chemicals called neurotransmitters. These neurotransmitters – such as serotonin, dopamine and acetylcholine – lead to a greater sense of wellbeing and creativity. Testosterone, the sex hormone associated with greater bone and muscle strength in women, also leads to increased risk-taking. We're more likely to want to start a new project, look for a new job or feel better about joining a new team during this time.

*Then we reach the peak of our menstrual cycle, ovulation, or our inner **summer**.*

Our oestrogen levels have peaked and we're starting to ride the wave of progesterone, the sex hormone that's released when we ovulate. We'll feel like our best selves during this time, with bags of confidence and strong communication and negotiation skills. This is the best time to pitch for a new piece of business, negotiate a salary increase or have the appraisal you prepared for during your inner winter. This confidence will also mean that we'll feel more social and collaborative, even those of us who are introverted. It's tempting to try to do as much as possible during this time of peak energy. But it's important to remember that our energy is akin to a bank account: we make deposits and withdrawals. If we're doing too much without allowing for corresponding times of rest, this can lead to us feeling depleted (or in an energetic "overdraft") right before and during our periods.

Finally, we get to the last phase, the luteal, or inner **autumn.**

Most of us associate this time with PMS; however, with reframing, we can harness the cyclical changes to our advantage. Firstly, we can split this phase into two parts: early and late luteal, similarly to the way early autumn (September to mid-October) feels different to late autumn (mid-October to November). During the early luteal phase, we're still feeling the highs of the peak of oestrogen and the peak of progesterone. This means we'll have sustained energy, and we'll want to be focused on current projects, rather than starting anything new. As we move toward the end of our menstrual cycle into our late luteal phase, naturally declining oestrogen and progesterone means that we'll start to move into what I call "get shit done" energy: a need to complete what's on our to-do lists and wrap things up, so we can do less during our periods and feel okay with that.

Looking at our menstrual cycle as a whole, we see that everything is connected. What we do in one part influences the next. We can use this knowledge to our advantage, allowing us to move away from a masculine 24-hour structure to one that incorporates all the powerful changes that happen through our entire menstrual cycle.

Full moon ritual

The full moon is a mystical and exciting time for intention-setting. Every 28 days, you can use it as an opportunity to reflect on what you'd like to let go of, as well as what you'd like to bring more of, before the next full moon.

The ritual

- Get a pen and notepad.
- Position yourself near a window, or outdoors, with a view of the full moon.
- If indoors, you might like to light a candle. This signifies the start of your ritual.
- Now write out everything that has gone well in the past month; everything you'd like to celebrate.
- Next, write about what you'd like to let go of, from the past month. This might be connected to people, place, moods, foods, routines, clients . . . anything. Pull this piece of paper out of your notebook and set it to one side.
- Lastly, write a list of everything you'd like to see, do and feel before the next full moon.
- You can now discard the piece of paper detailing what you'd like to let go of. Crumple it up, rip it to pieces or burn it on the fire (if you have one and if it is safe for you).
- Close your eyes and give thanks for all that has gone well. Bid farewell to all the stuff you're letting go and say that you are now ready to receive.
- Blow out your candle.

CONCLUSION

A s I write, it's just under a year since I left my parents, siblings and nephews in London and moved to Somerset with my husband and our three children. I was excited about the move – to be closer to nature; to have a new school better suited to our children's needs – but it was hard. After spending a couple of weekends with my family in London, I returned to Somerset feeling angry. I was resentful about having made the move away from my parents, as they are getting older (even though I actually see them more now, because they come and stay with us, so we get longer stretches of time together).

Anyway, I was back in Somerset, feeling bad, and I remembered that the next day I'd booked myself in for a massage in a yurt. The following morning, I drove up a bumpy dirt track and parked on the edge of some woodland, looking out over an open field. I walked up a path through the trees and came to a clearing. There was a beautiful yurt in the centre of it. I opened the door to go in and was welcomed by Claire, a kind and gentle soul. It was so warm inside, with a log burner heating the space.

We walked over to some cushions and rugs on the floor and sat together, cross-legged. Claire asked me how I was . . . and I burst into tears. I was surprised, I'm not usually so openly emotional. I told her about the sadness I was feeling, living further from my family. We talked about the nomadic imprint in my body, following years spent moving around and living in different places;

it's as if my body is expecting another move, she told me. Though it's not necessarily what it needs.

After talking, I lay on the massage bed and had a lovely, relaxing treatment. I felt my breath slow down and my shoulders drop. Human touch is crucial for our wellbeing. It calms our central nervous system and slows down our heartbeat. It also reduces blood pressure and cortisol (the stress hormone) and triggers the release of oxytocin (that love hormone that makes you feel amazing).

We sat together again after the massage and drank herbal tea. We talked more, then I went on my way. When I returned to my car for the drive home, I felt lighter. The yurt massage experience and time with Claire – a healer – helped to open me up. There was space for all my emotions, for me to share my imperfect life and the things I was finding hard.

This became an SQ-raising experience for me, because I was connected to nature, to a healer, I was touched by hands that made me feel calm and supported. It felt like a magical massage, like walking into a fairytale. In the wellbeing world, there's been a shift towards activities that are free and don't take up too much time and I get it: wellbeing shouldn't be exclusively for those who can afford it. But I also think that investing in yourself, occasionally, with something as wonderful as a healing massage from a person you feel safe with, really is worth it.

It was experiences like that yurt massage that made writing this book so blissful. At first, I worked slowly, punctuating my days with beautiful spiritual experiences that served as research: a Shamanic healing session that turned me into a bird in my mind (see page 241); several breathwork sessions (see page 24) that have both grounded me and helped me to transcend my body; sitting in a sauna with the smell of the wood and doing nothing except thinking. I needed to be raising my own SQ while teaching you how to raise yours, because if I'd been writing in a state of panic, that would have come through in the text. Ideas would have been lost; stories would have felt rushed. So, without even thinking about it consciously, I embarked on the most balanced, harmonious and magical book-writing journey.

As my book deadline approached, I wrote faster, worked harder and kept my head down. But I continued to take walks in nature; to dip my hands in natural spring water while walking through ancient woodland; to take time for my version of prayer and to make music, which is a high SQ creative process for me. My focus remained so clear that the writing never felt difficult.

Towards the end of writing the book, though, I needed a break. I pressed "save", emailed myself the document I'd been working on – superstitiously – and lay on the floor of my office. I started to breathe in and out through my nose, using the rhythm of a breathwork playlist I found on Spotify. As the tempo picked up pace, so did my breathing. Soon, I was breathing deeply and heavily, in and out of my mouth; exhaling as though I was sighing or even growling. It didn't matter, I was alone and it felt good.

While laying there, my whole body tingling, I found ideas dropping into my mind for this book; stories I'd forgotten to include. And then I called for support. I asked that the book reach people all around the world; I said I want to spread this message far and wide. And I gave thanks. I said: "What do you have to tell me?" And my grandma appeared in my vision. It felt as though she was saying: "You're not alone." I cried. I felt my body vibrating with the oxygenation; I felt emotions flood through me.

Now, I couldn't have included this experience in the introduction to this book because, until you have raised your own SQ – which hopefully, by now, you have – it wouldn't make sense. I've read books that open with ecstatic dance and transcending your reality and I've thought: *What on Earth are you talking about? You've lost me before we've even begun.* So I wanted to enter this SQ subject slowly and carefully before flinging my arms open and saying: "Right, you're ready to hear it, you're ready to receive, let's go: WOO!"

And while doing my breathwork meditation, I remembered a story and I wanted to share it with you, to end this book.

If you ask people about spirituality or spirits, you'll find that some people are totally open to it, others aren't quite sure but will be keen to hear what you have to say . . . and then there's a third camp who say they believe nothing. Except they always have just one story of spirituality that they do believe. My own husband wouldn't have described himself as spiritual prior to me writing this book and sharing practices with him (now, he tells me he's opening up to it). He still says he doesn't believe in "ghosts" or energies. Except, that is, for the one in the farmhouse he grew up in. That one is real, he says. The crying lady who has been heard by various family members and friends, in the middle of the night, over the past few decades. I stay quiet and nod, smiling. *So you don't believe in spirits except when you do*, I think.

There's another story that my brother-in-law, Denis – a science teacher – tells. Denis is also adamant that there is nothing in this world beyond what has been proven by science. Except just this one time when spirituality called a mother to her child. Denis's mother grew up in Australia and spent a lot of time outdoors with her sister and their friends. One day, someone they knew was working out in the fields and that person suddenly felt a need to rush home. There was a voice telling them to go, *right now*. They got back to a child who needed their help. Denis's mother and her siblings explained this by saying that people were more in touch with the land back then. There were fewer external factors to overload the senses, so people could be more in touch with their feelings and what was going on around them. The story is testament to the power of nature, and our spiritual connection to it.

At the start of this journey, Megan – my agent – kept asking me for explanations about various aspects of spirituality I wanted to write about. "But why does it make you feel that way?" she'd ask. "How does it work?" This stuff is so engrained in me that it was hard to explain. "It just is" I'd want to say . . . before remembering that – as a writer – it's my job to explain what sometimes feels inexplicable. When I wrote phrases such as, "It's believed that . . ." or "Some think that . . ." Megan would say: "Claim it. You know this stuff." And so I did. I am. I do know about SQ because I do it, believe it, live it, love it, share it. And I hope that, now, you will too.

Writing this book has been the most humbling, profound and beautiful experience. I'm so grateful for the opportunity. I wish you well on your SQ journey. I hope you unlock magic, meaning, connection, purpose, joy, contentment and all the other wonderful things that I've been gifted by these practices.

Annie x

"Realize deeply that the present moment is all you have. Make the now the primary focus of your life." Eckhart Tolle

APPENDICES

SQ instruments

Tibetan singing bowl
I have mine on my desk and I give it a "dong" at the start of the day, while setting an intention, and another at the end of the day, to mark the day closing and give thanks for all the work that was achieved.

Hang drum
This has been on my vision board for around 14 years, since I worked for a record label with a hang drum artist. It's yet to materialize, but this is the most beautiful instrument to create rhythms, melodies and to sing and meditate with.

Chimes
I have wind chimes in the garden. When I walk through and hear them tinkling in the wind, it offers an opportunity to be still, present and grateful for both nature and the music they make.

Bells
In my home, we have a very old set of servant's bells that are – obviously – no longer in use. But I like that I can still ring them and hear the resonant sound flowing through the house. Bells

feel welcoming (like a doorbell) and serve as a reminder that you have company.

Voice

You can use your voice to chant, shout, sing, create harmonies – when singing with others – and recite poetry. Your voice can be such a powerful instrument and it's with you wherever you go.

Shop for your SQ toolkit

These are some of my favourite SQ shops to visit in person. You can arrange a pilgrimage, if you don't live nearby, or have a look at the websites.

She's Lost Control, London

This is where I bought my first tarot deck. I was visiting my sister and we wandered in to admire the crystals and palo santo sticks. I found the *Starchild* tarot deck in there and it's still my favourite deck. The shop has a good website too, where you can order crystal candles, gems, tarot cards and more.

sheslostcontrol.co.uk

Star Child, Glastonbury

Glastonbury is full of witchy and spiritual shops – and well worth a visit – but this one is among the best. Candles, botanicals, essential oils, perfumes, incense, smudge sticks, big brightly coloured altar candles . . . It feels like stepping back in time. You can buy most things from the website, too.

starchild.co.uk

The Healing Hub, Frome

This place has a great selection of crystals that come with little notes on their properties and what you can use them for. Catherine Reeves, who runs the shop, also offers one-to-one crystal healing. I love the herb-infused bath salts and massage oils that they sell, too.

Instagram.com/thehealinghubfrome/

The Old Forge Fossil Shop, Lyme Regis

This one has a website, but you can't buy from it. So a pilgrimage it might need to be. There is something so spiritual about Lyme Regis: the seafront with its Cobb; watching the crashing waves. It is worth a day visit or, better yet, an overnight stay in one of the cottages on the seafront.

Fossilshop.net/index.html

Here are some SQ shops and websites recommended by my online community:

UK

- Lotus crystals, Galston (lotuscrystals.co.uk)
- Black Moon Botanica, Edinburgh (blackmoonbotanica.co.uk/)
- The Silver and Stone Shop, Castleton (bluejohnstone.com)
- Solstice, Holywood, Belfast (solsticeshop.co.uk)
- The Geordie Witch, Newcastle upon Tyne (thegeordiewitch.com)

USA

- houseofintuitionla.com
- queendomcultivation.com
- mysticelements.com

- riteofritual.com
- dreaminggoddess.com

Australia

- skcrystal.com
- thesacredwillow.com.au
- thewellbeingstore.com.au
- karma-living.com.au
- witchinwares.com.au

New Zealand

- thecrystalpoint.nz
- oceangypsy.co.nz
- consciouscrystals.co.nz
- rivendellshop.co.nz
- knightinspired.co.nz

SQ book recommendations

Rituals for Life: A guide to creating meaningful rituals inspired by nature by Isla MacLeod (Laurence King Publishing, 2022)

How to Tap the Magic Power in Incantations, Spells, Prayers & Psalms by Geoffrey B Samson (Finbarr Book Productions, 1981)

Candle Burning Magic: A spellbook of rituals for good and evil by Anna Riva (International Imports, 1980)

Folk Magic and Healing: An unusual history of everyday plants by Fez Inkwright (Liminal 11, 2019)

Just Breathe: Mastering breathwork for success in life, love, business and beyond by Dan Brulé (Enliven Books, 2020)

Your Healing Power: A comprehensive guide to channelling your healing energies by Jack Angelo (Piatkus, 2009)

Nature-Speak: Signs, omens and messages in nature by Ted Andrews (Dragonhawk Publishing, 2004)
Journey to the Dark Goddess: How to return to your soul by Jane Meredith (Moon Books, 2012)
The Heroine's Journey: Woman's quest for wholeness by Maureen Murdock (Shambhala Publications, Inc, 2020)
Wild Mercy: Living the fierce and tender wisdom of the women mystics by Mirabai Starr (Sounds True, 2019)
The Secret by Rhonda Byrne (Simon & Schuster, 2006)

ACKNOWLEDGEMENTS

Thank you to Megan Staunton, my agent, who saw something in me and this book idea and got the ball properly rolling. It's such a treat to have you with me on this journey. And to Briony Gowlett, my editor at Radar, whose enthusiasm and encouragement have been so heartening. Not only did Briony see the magic of SQ and why this book needed to be published, but she also delivered first draft feedback in the most excitable, positive and beautiful way. A real skill. I'm grateful to Pauline Bache, Mel Four and everyone else at Radar and Octopus involved in the proofing, design and publication of *Raise your SQ*.

I'd like to thank my husband, Rich, for always supporting and believing in me. The fact that you are now engaging with your spirituality because of this book is mind-blowingly wonderful. My sister, Lauren Davies, is a constant source of inspiration in terms of how she sees and engages with the world, and her incredible design skills have helped me to create the digital platform raiseyoursq.com. My other sister (-in-law), Kerry Davies, is always inspiring me with her deep-rooted spiritual beliefs and how she shows up in the world, plus she brings out the best in my lovely brother, Joe. We're grateful to have you in our lives. Also, Mum and Dad: the foundations of it all. Thank you.

Over the years, I have met so many incredible spiritual practitioners: thank you to all of you for the lessons you've shared. Also, to my original spiritual sister Lizzie Hilton, with whom I made a pilgrimage to India aged 18. What a magical experience. And to my new spiritual sisters Rebecca Ferguson and Claire Frances. It's been such a delight to talk "SQ" with you both and to learn about new spiritual paths to explore. As we often say: it was always meant to be. Also to Tamu Thomas, my friend – featured in the introduction – who gently nudged me back onto my own spiritual path. I'm forever grateful. And my other wonderful women friends – old and new – you are all so appreciated.

Lastly, thank you to my children – Joni, Bodhi and Rudi – whose curiosity, wonderment and creativity remind me, daily, of what a joy it is to be alive.

ABOUT THE AUTHOR

Annie Ridout is the author of three non-fiction books, a journalist for the national press, a certified life coach and a business consultant. She has helped thousands of women to launch and grow online businesses through courses and coaching and now, Annie is sharing her secret SQ tips for more joy, magic and success – both at home and at work.